Snowbird Secrets

A Guide to Big Mountain Skiing

by

Jackson Hogen

&

"Guru" Dave Powers

Acknowledgements

In an echo of Pascal's wager, let's begin by thanking Hidden Peak. (The wise man chooses to believe.) Next in line for a lifetime supply of gratitude is the Dude, our angel, who fired this arrow from a single lift ride in March of 2012. No Dude, no book. This axiom is equally true of the co-authors: "Guru" Dave couldn't have written this book by himself, and Jackson couldn't have possibly written this book without the Goo. Embellishing our efforts are the excellent photographs from Powder Shots, Eric Hostetler, Jay Dash, Jeremy Bernard, Snowbird and our own Goo.

The line that stretches behind us is full of touchstone figures too numerous to mention here. For Jackson, John Fry provided inspiration and instruction, a lighthouse along ski journalism's rocky shore. Stu Campbell showed that the best instruction was the simplest, a legacy that lives on in the work of John Clendenin and Mike Rogan. Dave Fields demonstrated the charm of loyalty over time and circumstance. Tom Corlett, Joe Campisi, Frank Scott, Andy Bigford, Dave Bertoni, Greg Stump, Peter Keelty, the entire Snow Country test team and everyone who ever gave me an assignment when I so desperately needed it, helped make this moment possible. I am eternally grateful to you all.

For Dave, the roster of mentors runs deep, beginning with parents John and Betty Powers. They sacrificed to make skiing a big part of growing up and continued their unconditional support of my unconventional lifestyle of full-time skiing. The Fletchers of Nashoba Valley fueled the inspiration that got me here. A tip of the hat to Corky Fowler and Jim Wilder for taking the time to share their insights when I was a lost and clueless newbie. Junior Bounous epitomizes the grace, style and agelessness that I have tried to emulate. Enduring thanks to Mark Jones, who spent so much time getting my hands in the right place and still rips the hill like he was 20. And special gratitude to Todd Howard for being a fellow esoteric who articulates the deep insights of being that have shown me the unlimited depth of the sport.

A single paragraph shall enshrine our unspeakable thanks to our most intimate support team, Connie for Dave, Stephanie for Jackson.

Before we send you on your path to self-discovery, we must give a tip of the hat to Scot Schmidt, Tim Petrick, Pam Fletcher, Mike Hattrup, Joe Cutts, Paul Hochman, Doug Sabanosh and the sweet, extinguished lights of Doug Coombs, Jim Jack and Shane. Our appreciation for all the folks that make Snowbird tick is bottomless, with special recognition due to the patrol who make the hill safe and are always there when you need them. We bow reverently before the entire staff at the Forklift for their mid-morning ministrations and loving vibrations. Finally, our thanks to all the friends who over the years have shared our passion for this place. Whether you ski here every day or only once a year, whenever you're here it's as if all your friends are here too, in a place you never really left. Thanks for skiing with us.

Table of Contents

Courtesy of Powder Shots

Snowbird Secrets
A Guide to Big Mountain Skiing

Introduction

This is not a ski book in any conventional sense. It's not an instruction manual, although it certainly is intended to teach. It doesn't focus on famous personalities, unless you are generous enough to include its authors in that number. And while it's most decidedly about place, it's not intended to serve as an exhaustive guide to Snowbird. Snowbird Secrets is a collection of lessons learned by skiing big mountains, as taught by big mountains.

The organizing force in each chapter is an idea, a primordial theme that we believe will help skiers re-imagine their relationship with the mountain. After a brief exploration of how the idea applies to skiing, we guide you down that section of the mountain that teaches the lesson of the meditation. Any athletic, kinesthetically capable person who embraces the meaning of even one of the twenty-two meditations can accelerate to elite ability in a matter of hours.

Yet the point of each chapter isn't technique or mechanics, but appreciating a concept that applies beyond the borders of the White World. The mountain, in particular Snowbird's Hidden Peak in winter, provides the specific slopes and conditions where the idea intersects with our lives. Once we take you to the doorstep of some fabulous run, we can't very well just leave you there. So we demonstrate how the concept applies by coaching you down what can be a daunting proposition.

For make no mistake, a big mountain in winter can be a forbidding place. It pays to be humble and aware. Our purpose in occasionally taking you places you might never think of going on your own isn't meant to shock or intimidate but to instruct: we pick runs and conditions that evoke the lesson, and if that involves a brush with fear it's because that is when the lesson will be most valuable.

While the lesson of each chapter is meant to apply universally, the fact that every teaching is grounded somewhere along the circular aspects of Snowbird is no accident. Snowbird Secrets is very much the product of this particular mountain, and we do not mean that as some trope. This mountain and no other brought the authors together and schooled us in its ways, training us to write this book. We are simply doing as instructed.

While our lessons are grounded in this very special hill, they're transferrable to any big mountain. Sorry, little mountains, we love you, but a small hill just can't generate the energy field of a peak that rises over 3,000 feet. Big mountains are wilder, more primal, more unlike our everyday world. Sometimes they are scary, and we recount herein some hairball situations that are more Tim Burton than Walt Disney. That's why big mountains are different: they are less predictable, more demanding and therefore so much more rewarding.

We didn't want our meditations to be based on the moveable sand of fiction, but manifested on a very real mountain in very specific circumstances. To fully expand our message beyond skiing, wherever we take the reader, skiing has to be rooted in reality. As we move between the metaphysical and the physical, we want the latter to be as concrete as we can make it. So at some point in each meditation we go on the mountain to show where and how the teaching comes into play in context. This is where the Goo's thousands of runs of experience serve as our guide.

When we refer to the power of vortices, the irrefutable evidence of the Fibonacci sequence, or the connections between sounds, geometry and colors, we're not reciting New Age incantations. The link between the physical and metaphysical is revealed in the language of reality, also known as the laws of nature. All we're doing here is making observations supported by math and physics as presently understood. You can consider it fanciful, if that's what you would normally call the application of math to observation of the natural world. Before dismissing our conclusions, skeptical readers are encouraged to further investigate the science.

What the mountain guided us to create was a portal through which you could see the invisible energy that surrounds us. The visible light we can see is only a tiny fraction of the energy in the air, which is a very busy place. Electromagnetic pulses, microwaves, cell phone conversations, TV shows, sports-talk radio, neutrinos, sounds beyond our hearing and other undetectable vibrations are omnipresent in the atmosphere. Yet the most powerful invisible energy remains the idea.

The creation of anything new begins with an idea. Before making a turn or picking a line comes the idea. And so we have built this book around themes or concepts. We hope you bring them into your heart as well as your mind, and let them infuse your skiing. For you're still the pilot, the vessel for the idea's expression, the quiet fulcrum, the seat of power from which you unleash your personal frequency.

Skiing consists of making a series of incomplete circles that somehow feel whole. We know circles are meant to be round and closed, or if not, then a spiral, a circle formed in time. Somewhere that cycle of energy is being completed. It's our contention the mountain completes our turns by absorbing our incomplete arcs and sending their energy back through us. When we move in cadence with the mountain we are repaid with interest for the energy we invest.

Skiing isn't just exercise. It's not like going for a walk, or running after a ball. In what other sport are you led to discover not only that all space is curved but that time is elastic? Skiing is an opportunity to step into gravity's stream and find yourself before you reach the other shore.

If the idea of stepping into an invisible energy field sounds wacky, consider this: speed fliers step into the invisible air above mountains and ride the vortices that swirl just above them all the way to the valley floor. The air may be invisible, but it's definitely not empty.

Snowbird Secrets is written in one voice but it's the product of two minds and two lifetimes devoted to skiing. "Guru" Dave Powers has spent thousands of days exploring this mountain and all it means. Most likely he doesn't even hold the record for most days skied here, despite logging more than 100 days a year since 1976. But no one has a deeper understanding of *why* he has come here than the Goo. Jackson Hogen has been called here almost every year since 1978. The two missed years were lessons in why not to miss another. The gifts of this mountain can never be repaid, but these words are Jackson's attempt to express his gratitude.

With everyone's kind indulgence, Jackson needs to pull back the veil on our dual authorship and speak in the first person singular for a spell. It's the shortest path to telling you just what you hold in your hands. On March 13, 2009, I died. Due to a medical condition that I would be reluctant to discuss with doctors in private and therefore shall not share in the public forum, I passed out cold while driving east on I-80. It was around rush hour on a Friday afternoon, I was travelling with the flow at around 65mph or so when I lost all consciousness. The car drove on, unsupervised for anywhere from one to two minutes, with the Truckee River an easy leap to the right and no bailout left. Somehow the SUV continued onward unmolested, traversed a seemingly impassable median and crossed every lane of on-coming, weekend-bound traffic, coming peacefully to rest with no more than a few scratches.

How many angels it took to carry me across five lanes of traffic I don't know. At the time, I only knew that something remarkable had just happened, but I couldn't fathom the significance. Why save me? My life was of no particular consequence. I spent another two years ignoring all the signals the universe was sending me to stop what I was doing and focus on this.

I didn't know why I was saved from certain extinction until the day I sat down to write this book. As prelude to what I am about to divulge, allow me to share that I have been paid to write all sorts of twaddle for around 25 years and have never experienced anything approaching this. Day after day, after writing for a few minutes, a pillar of fire would open the top of my skull and pour energy down through me like I was a funnel. It was like having a celestial battery hooked to either end of my body and someone turning on the juice. I'm surprised my hair wasn't smoking.

The energy out of my fingertips was convulsively powerful, light guiding consciousness. Columns of what I felt as light coursed through me, igniting emotions, charging the mind to grasp the words and get them down. When the passage would be complete I would be exhausted and it would take some time as we know it for me to cool off. What I discovered when I revived and read what had been channeled through me, were the most perfect jewels I ever felt flow from the ether to the page. Some powerful juju wanted Dave's message to come through me.

In the process, I came to realize I wrote this with Dave because the mountain brought us together for this purpose, that each was chosen for his gifts. When we go on the mountain on these pages, it's the Goo who guides us. This really is his book, although the final turns of phrase are mostly channeled through my keyboard. But that was my job, the part I could do. *I did not expect any of this*, not a word. I would say I had nothing to do with it, but that isn't right either. I was chosen, I was the one able to show up, and for that I am eternally grateful.

It may sound like hubris or idiocy to say so, but we sincerely believe that the making of this book was no accident, nor was there any coincidence in the authors' intertwined history that led to our mind-meld. Why it took so long for these messages to find this particular expression we cannot say, except to suggest that spirit doesn't share our worries about time.

Before sending you on to the real business of this book, we want to share one more thought that we found in the energy that inspired it. The great medieval Aristotelian philosopher Averroes wrote that proper teaching should communicate on the sensual, intellectual and spiritual levels. How well we have succeeded in attaining this ideal is for you, Dear Reader, to say, but our hope is that you find in these pages the pleasure of language, the understanding of clear minds and the joy of pure, undiluted spirit, also known as love.

Looking down on Hidden Peak

Looking down on Hidden Peak

Orientation

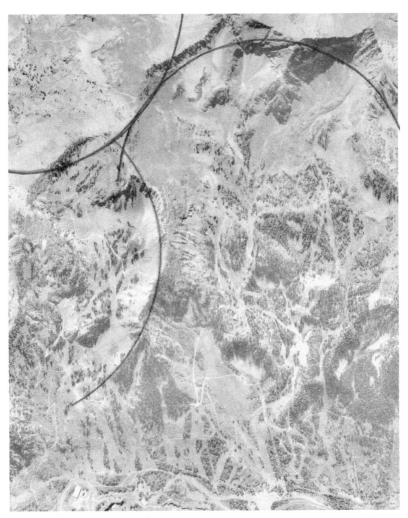

The 3 vortices of Hidden Peak converge precisely at its summit.

Chapter 1

On Aspects
&
The Meaning of the Mountain

As you stand in the Plaza looking up the tramline at the mountain, you are facing south, which in the White World means the slope faces north. To the east, up the canyon, lies Alta, while the road down to the valley travels west. While this is useful knowledge, you now know as much about Snowbird as medieval European cartographers knew about America. To begin to understand this place you need to take it all in from a global perspective, so let's climb up to 12,000 feet and take a look back down.

What you will see are three gigantic amphitheaters carved out of rock and crystal, each containing within its circumference nearly 360° of exposure. These nearly-closed circles overlap exactly at the top of Hidden Peak, the energy epicenter from which gravity's stream spills in all directions. Any circle on a mountain perforce exists in three dimensions, turning a circle into a spiral, the vortex that invariably assumes the whirlpool shape of the Fibonacci sequence.

The primary lesson to your orientation is the understanding that you have three major gravity funnels at your disposal: Peruvian Gulch, Gad Valley and Mineral Basin. The key to divining which of the three to select and where to attack it – the practical application of the fundamental problem of where to be in space at any given moment in time - lies in awareness of the microclimates that prevail along each aspect, which are defined by wind, sun, elevation, traffic, time of season and the pitch of the slope. By thinking in terms of aspect, on any given day you can find the best snow on the hill because with so much terrain, facing so many directions, the snow is bound to be good somewhere. Let's go find it.

One factor that never pulls its punches throughout the long season is the wind. Prefrontal winds are generally out of the south and southwest, meaning the wind will be transporting snow from these aspects and depositing them in the adjacent aspects. For example, a south wind will strip the west-facing Regulator Johnson clean, but the beneficiaries will be a filled-to-choking Upper Cirque and all like leeward faces along the Middle Cirque.

When a big storm moves in, the wind often switches to the northwest, which will begin mining the north-facing sections, relocating the goods to eastern and southern faces such as Mineral Basin, the Lower Cirque, and some of the south-facing aspects in both Gad Valley and Peruvian Gulch. As accumulation builds up, it's subject to scorching by the wind, creating breakable wind slab, as challenging a condition as you ever want to encounter. West-facing shots get the most damage from the wind, but northern aspects can also be suspect. Knowledge of the prevailing wind direction over the past 24 hours will tell you where to look for freshness.

Mineral Basin, east- and north-facing aspects

Mineral Basin, south aspect

The best time to catch wind-deposited fluffulescence is while the white gold is in transit from one aspect to another. On a storm day, you can keep returning to the same shot and the wind will have already repaired the damage caused by your last tracks just one run ago. The snow bank keeps taking fresh deposits from the wind and carelessly leaves them out for us to pilfer.

Snowbird is comprised of three giant turbines perched on the edge of a wind-inducing canyon. This means a wind that blows out of the south on the upper mountain will circle back a few hundred feet lower to attack from the north. It may take some exploration, but it's usually possible to find continually smooth lines top to bottom by reading the circular wind flow. If the wind is moving with such force that all terrain features have been obliterated, it's time to head to the trees, natural snow collectors that do not easily surrender their stockpile of the essence. The essence is what we came for, the extraordinary aggregation of millions of water crystals, the uniqueness of each suggesting they're animated by free will, the fractal forms they assume as inevitable and unalterable as destiny.

Early in the season, the sun sits low in the sky during its brief appearance in the frigid skies, minimizing its effect on snow quality. As the sun climbs higher in the sky as the season progresses, it becomes a significant factor in snow quality very quickly. Given the sun will arise in the east, it sets to work first on east-facing exposures in Mineral Basin, then swings southward, eventually striking western slopes. It's not until very late in the season that the sun has much effect on the northern exposures that dominate the front face of the mountain. Before spring, the cold snow on these north faces will remain soft and pliable for days after other aspects are cooked to a crisp. In the fullness of spring, the sun rules the choice of aspect selection. By following the circular path of the sun, you can ride the swell of goodness as it ripples around the aspect dial.

Unfortunately, ignorance of aspects is an uninsurable offense. There may be no immediate recourse from a heinous route selection that leaves you marooned on a giant slab of something slicker than blubber yet more bulletproof than Kevlar. The only remedy for error is awareness of aspect, and the mercy is how small a change can change everything.

When White Diamonds gets a grooming makeover in the spring, the swath of sweetness can't be more than 40-feet wide, yet the skier's-left side is firmer underfoot, almost greasy, while the softer snow on the right side flakes off the edge like the flesh of freshly poached fish, proving again that the choice of aspect is critical right down to the finest segment of the circle. Just a half-degree slice of the $360°$ pie can be silken while on either side lays incorruptible rubble.

Elevation is another key consideration in evaluating aspect options. In the early season, an inversion will make it colder at lower altitudes than it is on the peak, so what might be velvety up high evolves into something much firmer down low. Later in the season, the upper sections stay frozen longer and the lower elevations break earlier.

Once conditions deteriorate on the softening lower mountain, move to higher ground, following the sun's wake as it moves across the compass.

Remember, a very small change in the aspect can make a huge difference in the same zone. Along the Middle Cirque you may think you're looking at a continuous aspect, but if you look closely you'll see that just along the sign line that marks the beginning of the Lower Cirque is a facet turned slightly to the northeast, while below this same fall line the terrain twists to a southeast aspect. One moment you're styling on dry chalk, but if you don't see that elevation has changed your aspect, in a few hundred feet you'll be a pawn in a game of breakable crust chess.

Terrain features like knolls, rolls, guts, and spines can also have a full 180° of aspect change in a very short space. You can find a smooth creamy line right next to a fight-for-survival condition. Less than a degree of aspect change can load one line with nectar, but wind-slab its neighbor. Anyone can make a mistake when the line between genius and folly is so fine, even a guru. The gospel of the mountain is that if you do make a bad call, redemption may be only a few feet away. Find a slight change in aspect and you might find what you were looking for in the first place.

Slope angle is another major contributor to aspect quality, especially in the spring. A steep, north-facing shot might be fast and hard, but as the pitch flattens out at the bottom, where the snow surface has absorbed a lot of sun, it's soon going to get ski-stopping sticky, creating a problematic situation. If you have a feeling the flats ahead may have turned to congealed oatmeal, spill some heat so that you can negotiate the stickiness factor without going over the handle bars.

Nothing aids orientation like being able to see where you are. One of the many beauties of Hidden Peak is it affords a view of what's happening in the vortices that swirl off its apex. A hard, reflective glaze off the snow on Little Cloud informs you in advance of its perils; the evidence of wind-scour on Silver Fox can be read from the tram or Peruvian chair. Take in your surroundings every chance you get, for the time will come when sight will be a sense no longer served. When visibility plummets, dousing every detail with undifferentiated white, all you have left is your knowledge of where you stand and where the aspect that contains you will lead. Your choices will be down to two: find some trees so you can tell which way is up, or feel the invisible cadence of the hill, trust it, and ski.

Learn to see the spirals in the terrain and the cycles of sun and wind. Try to channel the hill's intentions. For make no mistake, this mountain is talking to you and you can hear it if you will only calm down and listen. Let's go back up to 12,000 feet and see what else altitude has to tell us about the mountain's message.

Looking down, the circular patterns are as clearly etched as crop circles. Hidden Peak is revealed as the epicenter of a giant, vertically oriented circle that contains within it three circular funnels, each of which capture the cyclical movements of the sun along their nearly 360° aspects. If you complete all the circles in your mind's eye, you'll notice a resonance with the pattern of circles within circles known in sacred geometry as the Flower of Life. Whether you believe that this ancient symbol carries with it talismanic powers doesn't matter. The proof of this mountain's sacred power is that you are here. This place does not call you by accident but by intent. And once you are here, you are part of the flow whether you care to be or not.

While an aerial view of the mountain doesn't show the intricate, 19-circle pattern of the Flower of Life in its customary, two-dimensional precision, Snowbird is very much a 3-D world, multiplying its tri-petal pattern through myriad planes. A mountain may appear like a static object, but movement lives here every moment in the guise of gravity's stream. This mountain is alive with energy, moving downhill through multifaceted funnels, imparting circularity to the energy, bound by the laws of nature to move in perfect harmony with the swirling Fibonacci pattern, mathematics moving through air.

When you step off the edge of the circle and into the gravity stream, you discover the hill has a beat. The topographic shapes of the sub-circles are like the patterns formed in crystals by musical tones: they emanate a rhythm, a flow they invite you to match. When you are blessed to discover a section of perfection, don't be in too much of a hurry to swig it in one shot. Sink into the sensation of velvet, luxuriate in the forces flowing through you, open the moment to feel the intimacy of your skis' curvature contacting curling corn snow.

Your turn frequency is part of the song of your soul. The beat you feel at the bottom of each turn sends sonar to the mountain that it returns with extra emphasis, adding propulsive power when it ought to be dissipating. Your strength grows with each centered, harmonizing arc; the mountain's secret is that you are an ion in its electric field, feeding its enormous crystal warehouse of energy. You become part of the loop, your being dissolving in the doing, rejuvenation wearing the party hat of recreation.

This is not a new idea. When Heracles was wending his way homeward after his eleventh labor – some business about golden apples in the Garden of the Hesperides, which proved deucedly difficult to find – he happened into Antaeus of Libya. Antaeus was the son of Gaia, the earth mother, so he gained strength every time he touched the ground. When we ski in harmony with the hill, we become like Antaeus, drawing energy from the earth every time we throw ourselves against it. (Antaeus, as patriarchal myth would have it, was a nasty sort; Heracles killed him by holding him off the ground.)

The story of aspect reveals the meaning behind the mountain because it's the unifying idea that explains the place, the interplanetary view that allows us to see the timeless rotation of energy around and through this multi-channel mountain. This is the stream we join, an endless feedback loop we participate in every time we drive into the hill and extract more energy out than we gave.

The mountain absorbs our energy and feeds it back to us. A lovely metaphor, yes, only we aren't speaking metaphorically. Snowbird, you see, under its rock crust, is a giant mass of quartz, which like all crystals generates harmonic energy. It is also a piezoelectric collector and conductor of all the energy to which it's connected, a field that includes us. Somehow we find significance in joining the energy this mountain emanates. Perhaps it's our nature that seeks meaning in the most minor of details. Perhaps it's the awareness that nowhere else can our being dissolve in the doing, where we can disappear on one plane and reappear, as pure bliss, on another. Just as the connection between time and the eternal lies in the infinitesimal moment, so does the connection between the metaphysical and the physical lie in the minutia of now, a present where we discover the elasticity of time, still in the eye of the hurricane, cradled in the center of an arc.

Looking up Peruvian Gulch

Crystal ridges of corduroy ready to release their signature vibration.

Great Scott, Upper Cirque

Great Scott as it appears from its doorstep

Chapter 2

DANCING IN
The Gravity Stream
BECOMING
The Eye of the Storm
BEING IN
The Slow-Motion Moment of Now

Physicists consider gravity a weak force because, compared to magnetism or the energy that holds atoms together, its power is piddling. When applied to humans on skis, however, gravity has more than enough oomph to propel one to speeds where the mind can no longer process events. Ingrained, appropriate responses must already be pre-programmed if one is going to go dancing in the gravity stream.

Low-angle slopes impart the impression that, like you, gravity is on vacation. It's a gentle giant, holding you sweetly in its arms, cradling you down the hill. You might agree with the physicists and conclude gravity is a weak force when you're cruising the blue runs of Colorado, but there's no mistaking its powerful presence once you are two turns into Great Scott. The gravity that permanently resides on the steeps crowning the Upper Cirque is all business and charging its maximum day rate.

To find your way in, toddle off the tram in the direction of Regulator Johnson. Just past the snow fence at the top of Regulator, immediately cut right through the gate. If you are going to step into gravity's stream here, be ready for the rush. Because it's steep and slightly twisted, the entrance to Great Scott may be marred by choppy bumps, but this gnarly debut is followed by an uninterrupted fall line that feels like you're skiing the face of Niagara Falls. If you can summon the nerve to charge the chop at the top so you carry speed into the first unimpeded turn, you will learn what it means to become the eye of the storm.

If you catch Great Scott or any of the adjacent shots that dot the Upper Cirque when there are two feet of fresh-as-innocence powder, you will have a chance to form your own weather system. Commit to the fall line with all you have or will ever have and set up a rhythm even a white boy can dance to. With the first full turn, the snow churn off your prow punches you in the chest, but this is only prelude. Shift your balance to your arches, press against what lies ahead, and the flumes of snow that your skis tear out of the slope will curl completely over your head. You are the center, the soul and the entirety of a universe of one, balanced because you have to be, because it's who you are at that moment.

At the bottom of each turn your feet reach for a reality that you have to create, following a path that is beyond second-guessing. Hell, there's no time for first-guessing. You are the Autopilot Kid, moving with a rhythm that has been on the planet longer than we have. The wave flies over your head, broken only by the millisecond that you pull your babies across the fall line into yet another controlled fall in gravity's reckless embrace.

Who is doing this? It can't be your conscious mind because that puppy can't keep up with this chain of events. If you have to reason your way down Great Scott on a storm day you will have many non-harmonious moments. You have to have seen this movie before, if only in your head. It also helps to have an adrenalin rush, although if on pow day you are one of the first few skiers into Great Scott and you *don't* have an adrenalin rush, see your doctor immediately. You may not be alive.

Like so many of Snowbird's iconic descents, Great Scott has enough room to be shared. It raises the adrenalin ante when you have a buddy alongside, each knowing there's only room for two perfect sets of tracks between the avalanche slag skier's left and rope line skier's right and you both charge it like Blue Angels, just out of each other's wash, side-by-side. The world is going by very, very fast, but there is so little going on inside the eye of the storm – just a casual do-si-do back and forth – that time warps. Speed you don't feel is speed you don't fear.

Inside your cocoon, the snow funnel you create as gravity's wedge, you are aware of the chaos around you yet are so focused on the moment that the moment opens up. Time elongates. You feel the microseconds of a ski's fall through snow with the resistance of oxygen until you sense a bottom where there is no bottom and ride the energy back the other way. Now you understand what Kierkegaard meant when he wrote that the moment is the connection to the eternal. When totally immersed in the Now you become somehow disconnected from it, for there is nothing else, not even time.

At moments like this, you won't survive if there is a schoolmarm in your head barking some catechism of technique. Even if the instruction happens to be correct – a big if – its appearance now is unlikely to be of much help. If you do feel a wheel coming off, toss everything you have straight down the fall line and hope you've nipped the crisis in the bud, but doing so has to be an instinct rather than a decision discovered after internal debate or the debater will end up with his or her head under two feet of

Wasatch white. Point being, your mind, no matter how clever, can't keep up with a headlong charge down Great Scott. You have to bring something to this party, namely the ability to ride in the eye of the storm while you dance in gravity's stream.

Lest we be accused of peddling mumbo-jumbo to a credulous public, allow us to inject some practical advice for those who aren't adept at dancing in the stream. Once past the first couple of awkward turns at the entry to Great Scott, slip over to skier's right and stop. But don't tarry long. Quickly set up with your ski tails dug into the snow under you, your tips straight down the fall line. Look as far down the hill as you can, check your mirrors for incoming traffic, rock back and press forward hard, driving straight downhill and into the top of the first turn. When you feel the bottom and your feet start to rise on the ski's uncoiling energy, pull your feet up towards your butt and reset your skis' base angles to ride the wave back the other way. It's not like you do nothing, but nor do you do everything. You have to be sensitive to how your skis are angled against the snow and move your feet more or less in unison with the rhythm of your turns.

But you shouldn't be thinking about any of this *while* you're trying to master Great Scott. Think first, then ski. Visualize success then let your body do your thinking for you. If your mind has an obnoxious habit of providing unsolicited advice, put some rock and roll on in your head, something loud and energizing, and don't let the music stop until the hill has lost its pitch and you stand at the bottom, breathless but unbowed.

When you are immersed in the slow-motion moment of Now, you can't be anyplace else and anyone else can't be messing with you. Tearing a stunning crease into the face of the Upper Cirque comes at a price and the tariff is total presence. As the sages say, you have to be here now. No one else gets past the velvet rope into your private space. Not your overdue taxes. Not your perfectly lovely, yet somehow periodically annoying, spouse. Not your chatty boss who will talk to you about anything but your stagnant compensation. No one. When you give your all to Great Scott you get back the ineffable power of immersion in the moment, with each moment holding the key to forever.

Looking up the gut of Great Scott

Regulator Johnson to Big Emma

*The groomed boulevard of Regulator Johnson, viewed from the
top of Gad 2.*

Chapter 3

On Vibrations

If you tear the universe down into its most essential components, all you have left is light and vibration. The tiny squiggles of energy that form the foundation of the quantum world are the essence of emanation, infinitesimal moments of spin, the fractals that make up the circle of life. What is vibration but a curve moving through space? Looked at from the perspective of the most fundamental elements from which we - and everything else, known and unknown - are constructed, we were made to ski.

Can it be mere happenstance that the single property that underlies all existence is also the most vital ingredient in skiing? Not only do we, like vibrations, move on a curved path through space, but that we move at all is a function of the ski's ability to vibrate. We don't often think of them this way, but skis are made to slide, and vibration is a prerequisite for sliding. A ski that doesn't vibrate doesn't move; it might as well be a snowshoe. The reason that metal is an indispensible element in race skis isn't, as is popularly imagined, because metal makes the ski stiffer, but because only metal issues just the right harmonics to break the grip of suction at speed.

Ski designers know all about vibration. The best ones think of little else. How to stifle the noxious frequencies that perturb edge grip while allowing safe passage to the essential vibrations that allow the ski to glide? It's a conundrum every ski must solve to achieve the epiphany of the perfect descent. A case could be made that we are like our skis in this regard: we too must be able to filter out energy that impedes our purpose while channeling the primary energy that sustains us.

A vibration moves by rising and falling, rising and falling, a cycle of constant renewal. This describes our pattern of movement on the mountain, a cycle that takes us from bottom to top and back to the bottom in order to rise again. But unlike an innate hum, we have will, so we can manage the frequency of our descent to match our own internal harmonic. To do so, we draw on a well of energy we call gravity that is the mountain's reward for our heeding its call.

If you think we are drifting into the murky realm of malarkey, think about this: Hidden Peak is riddled with quartz. Quartz is a crystalline structure, and no ordinary crystal at that. Like all crystals, it not only responds to vibrations, it emits them. Quartz has piezoelectric properties that allow it to store electromagnetic energy and to conduct it. This mountain pulls a pulse from your energy stream and sends it back with interest, but it also skims off a transaction fee that it stores in its gargantuan energy vault.

It goes without saying the human eye, marvel that it is, is rather pathetic. There is so much it cannot see. We don't see air, we don't see the vibrations that move through it and we don't see any of the other energy it contains, like wind or microwaves. Imagine if we could see the electromagnetic force fields that swirl ceaselessly through this mountain of crystals. It would be more beautiful and baffling than the streaming code of *The Matrix*, tides of energy rushing through every skier and rider, diving down a funnel of energy into the mountain and cycling back in ever stronger beats, proving with every turn that perpetual motion is not only possible, it happens every day.

So what does the mountain do with all this energy? Ask Ted Johnson, who first laid out his plans for the resort on a map spread across a dining room table at the Alta Lodge. Ask Dick Bass, who poured enough energy and resources into the mountain to bankrupt a principality, suggesting the forces that compelled him were more spiritual than commercial. Ask the waitress in the Tram Bar or your fellow passenger on a chairlift: what brought you here? For Johnson or Bass, it couldn't have been the quality resort reviews for there was no resort to review; it had to be something else, more primal. As it turns out, everyone has a story for how they came to discover Snowbird, but no one knows the *reason*. Some have the vanity to think they picked the place, but the wisest know the place picked them.

That is the secret that Snowbird has slipped into our subconscious; deep down, we know we were summoned here. We just have to be reminded of it to remember, an echo of the Platonic notion that all knowledge is remembrance. In the modern world we are so divorced from our natural selves that you would think we'd have lost the power to hear a mountain call us. And indeed we have, but such is the enormous reach of this place that it can still stir the last seed within us that connects us to the energy that surrounds us every day yet we do not see. The resonance of that tiny, vibrating seed is what brings us here, to this extraordinary place, to stand in the heart of the energy flow.

Because we are human and frail, we naturally assume the reason we were called was to benefit us. We come here to step into gravity's stream and learn to disappear into it, and for this we are deeply grateful. We know we are the lucky ones. Lost in the endorphin bath, we forget we aren't the only ones with a motive. The mountain didn't send out its vibrations to pull us here for our benefit; the mountain did it for itself.

Hidden Peak is a spirit center because that is its nature. It called Johnson and Bass and all who followed it to nourish the quartz, to bring fresh energy to funnel downhill and recharge its massive battery. We think in our silly way that it's all about us, and in a way, it is. After all, we were chosen. We're the ones who showed up. In return for our presence, we are recharged and renewed as we become part of the energy flow that constantly streams through this mountain. If we open our hearts to it, we become better people. If we open our minds to it, we are clearer thinkers. If we open our spirit to it, we understand that we, too, are vibrations and light.

Vibrations move at a given frequency, a signature wavelength they can use to organize matter or light into a pattern. If you touch a vibrating tuning fork to a plate of crystals, the crystals will move into a precise, incorruptible pattern that *is* that note. Different vibrations applied to light we call colors, and while we can detect millions of shades, the seven basic colors – red, orange, yellow, green, blue, indigo and violet – correspond exactly and invariably to the seven notes of the scale. So vibration is light and light is vibration, throughout our visible range and beyond.

Let us take the lesson to the hill. No snow condition induces vibration like early-morning corduroy, before temperature and traffic can dull the sharp ridges left by the groomers. So off the first tram head directly to Regulator Johnson, the iconic, west-facing ballroom that inclines ever steeper as it rolls downhill. As you come off the road that marks the run's entry, the slightest sideward drift will induce a hum you can feel in your teeth. Your feet will feel like they're living directly over the subway. When you try to jam your edges in the fall-away pitch, the hum only grows louder and your feet put in a request for a change in ownership. Now is the time to remember that vibration is color we don't see, another shade of invisible light. So be light. Guide a gently pressured edge across the hill, knowing some drift is inevitable, and when the spirit moves you, add a dash of energy and edge angle and instantly segue to a weight shift and direction change. Will you be beautiful? Probably not. Will the vibration dissipate? No. But you will be managing both trajectory and speed, which should be enough to get the job done. Remember that this particular facet of the mountain is relentlessly long, so don't let your horses run for the barn or you'll be on Mr. Toad's Wild Ride.

When you come off the last, steep pitch, you have only to negotiate your way past the base of the Little Cloud chair to pick up the gentle, ego-boosting terrain of Bassackwards. Your methods are the same: be light, set the edge and switch directions. Because gravity's stream is running calmer now you can afford to play, altering the wavelength of your turns to match the vibrations emanating from the hill. After you pass the Mid-Gad restaurant on your right, you catch a road that wraps around until it deposits you on top of Big Emma, the widest boulevard on the Snowbird roadmap. Here the crystal ridges of the corduroy will perforce be softer, the vibration off the snow less strident. But the other vibrations, those that issue from far deeper in the mountain's core, they still send out their subtle, sonic message to find your center. What the vibration of the mountain is telling you is that like the mountain itself, you are also a cache and conduit of energy. You also are made of light and sound, born to follow a curve through space.

Mark Malu, Road to Provo

The end of the Road to Provo spills into Mark Malu

Chapter 4

On Anticipation

For two days we gorged on Wasatch powder as if we were shooting a documentary on the short, tragic life of new snow in this canyon. (All that was missing from our fantasy experience was Elle MacPherson on an early tram, but we digress.) Even after a powder smorgasbord that would have sated any freshies gourmand, we still looked up at the vast, glistening, uncut snowfield that crowns Little Cloud and dreamt, like any addict in the swoon of an epic binge, of the next fix.

One cannot determine when the rope that embargoes the Road to Provo is about to drop by the arrival of the first contingent of patrol; nor by the size of the gathering throng, who stare at the untouched powder acreage ahead of them with the unflinching concentration of zombies; but by *who* is gathering at the edges of the ropes. One cannot fool cognoscenti schooled by decades of breathing the cadence of this powder paradise. They know when the patrol who matter are on the move, men and women who slide toward the rope with intention and a hint of foreboding. They take positions by gates they know better than members of their own families.

Feet stomp all around, impatient, like horses fidgeting before a race or a charge into battle, everyone aware that in the next instant we will all move like a tide of refugees dashing for safe harbor, each taking the calculus of the other, judging trajectory and intent, as we move to our secret Eden.

For a moment the rope doesn't move. We do. We slither silently forward, stepping casually here and there, no rush, nothing to see here, we are not the droids you're looking for. Then the rope is *down* and a churn, like dropping chum in a shark tank, commences and the first twenty souls surge as one. Perfect. They seek the solace of early goods where the pitch is steep and the obstacles entertaining. They will be gone as quickly as they bolted out of the gate, just a puff of smoke to mark where they cut skier's right off the road. We glide on, stepping around citizens with other agendas, until, just twenty seconds after the frenzy, we are alone; ahead, the sinuous corridor of Mark Malu lies in our sites.

Heightened anticipation opens the endorphin floodgates as our cross-hill flight closes the gap between us and the shimmering, opalescent skin of Mark Malu, as bright, uncut and alive as the belly of a freshly caught fish. In conditions like these, the snow provides a natural decelerant so there is no need to pump the brakes before plunging into Malu's open slope. Gravity's insistent allure invites speed at the expense of unwarranted turning, begging us to unfurl long tendrils of tracks that flow in harmony with the hill's slowly twisting face.

Anticipation on the physical plane forges the connection between anticipation as a mental state and its reward in a positive outcome. In the heartbeat before your ski tips traverse the brink of the road and drop you on the trail, you set up for the transition in pitch and speed by shifting your body into the quiet center of the first turn, committing your core to the fall line and your attitude to riding gravity's stream. Your upper body stays ahead of the activities going on underfoot, as though your head and shoulders were in a time machine that is forever stuck on transporting you a few milliseconds into the future. As mental anticipation morphs into the events that both end it and redeem it, physical anticipation allows for the happy confluence between the two states. Anticipation feels like a form of time travel for if you do it well, it shifts you into the future. You take care of business before it happens.

The skill that best informs the body how to anticipate the next turn is visualization. See yourself committing to the turn early, tilting into it as you roll your skis onto a complementary angle. Snow flies everywhere but you are calm in the center of a white room that moves with the beat of the hill. On the open slope of Mark Malu you gobble up turns in giant gulps, swigging the whole hill in a few thrilling arcs. You're not sipping prissy nips of Champagne; you're slamming powder shooters. You stretch your mind to the bottom of the hill, creating a tension between you and your destination that snaps you, not just through the next turn, but through every turn that you anticipate between now and the end of the trail.

To work at peak efficiency, anticipation loves a bit of sensory input. Vision is particularly nice and its absence particularly debilitating when you can't read enough data from the tactile slap of ski against snow. It's normal for visualization skills to go haywire when you can't see squat; however, this is exactly when they can be most useful, those times when inner vision has to substitute for eyesight if for no other reason than the latter system is out of commission. The rules of anticipation do not change. The bones are stacked on the center of the energy underfoot as the upper body dives into the void. The feet feel the terrain and move over it, massaging its contours, not resisting it but yielding to it, drawing energy from it and moving on.

Imagine the ecstasy when every detail on the path ahead is illuminated by glorious sunlight! Now there is no wrinkle you cannot anticipate, no wall of snow you can't transform into part of the dance. So what if there are bumps as tall as Mini Coopers? So what if there are trees every few feet? So what if there are both, on a pitch that seems to get steeper on every turn? You anticipate. Watch, adapt, let your feet make independent decisions about braking and line selection. Keep your upper body calm, centered, balanced. What is under you is behind you. What you see ahead is now. The moment you live in is anticipation of the next.

Looking into Mark Malu

White Diamonds Downhill, Mineral Basin

White Diamonds Downhill

Chapter 5

On Being Early

There are few things in skiing that work quite as well as being early. Every powder addict in the world knows the advantage of being early to the lift line or on the first tram, for these are the only ways to assure first tracks. While there's no denying the allure of uncut powder pastures, being early has more to recommend it than just untrammeled lines. The mountain is all but empty, stripped clean of the clatter, clutter and yammering that will populate it in a few hours. The engines that will soon sweep the public uphill lie still. The snow underfoot is colder and squeaks louder when you walk on it. The fraternity of the early begins to gather as another ski day rustles to life.

There are two best-possible scenarios for being early at the Bird. The red carpet route consists of early trams, three of which may ascend before the 9:00 AM cable car opens its doors to the masses. Gaining passage on early trams is reserved for those who can afford the heady tariff, which keeps the exclusivity high and the body count low. Standing on the top of Hidden Peak at the first glow of dawn is worth the price of admission, particularly if someone else is paying.

It may be foot-stomping, arm-swinging cold, but the tingling anticipation of the special run to come warms from the inside.

The alternate ideal for being early entails another form of exclusivity, albeit a more democratic one. It's known as "inter-lodge," shorthand for "due to avalanche danger you can't leave your building [any building] until further notice." This divides the world into two unequal parts: those who will be skiing moments after inter-lodge is lifted, and those who will be barricaded below the canyon waiting for the road to open. When inter-lodge is in effect, no early tram travelers can poach the Bird's abundant powder fields, giving everyone first shot at face shots. There is no better time in the world to be early.

There is another way to be early, and it doesn't require the resources of a pasha or serendipitous housing. This opportunity to be early comes with every turn and is open to all. Yet precious few skiers avail themselves of it, content to drift aimlessly side to side, all the while convinced that because their skis are pointing somewhat east one moment and almost west a few beats later, they must have mastered the art of carving.

The single biggest differentiator between the advanced skier and the true expert is the latter's ability to get to the next turn early. There are several components to being early, each of which moves in concert with the others. The upper body must continue its constant projection down the hill and into the turn, the existential lean of faith that is a prerequisite for performance skiing. The uphill hand cues a shift in weight to the ski below it by reaching for the fall line. And the uphill ski begins to tilt on edge early, at the top of the arc, supporting your hurtling mass as it navigates gravity's stream.

The essence of getting to the turn early pertains at all slope angles and in every condition, but its clarity shines most brilliantly on freshly crafted corduroy with some samba to its rhythm.

The business of getting to the turn early has been somewhat compromised with the advent of rocker. While the essentials of body position don't change, the ski's ability to find snow at the top of the turn may be diminished by anywhere from a little to where did it go? The key is to apply the early edge angle and pressure regardless and let the ski design make the most of it. Some rockered skis will hook up from the tip almost as if there were no early rise in the ski forebody, while others will have their loose shovels bounce around like ferrets on meth when they don't have any soft snow to press against.

While it is always advantageous to be early when riding firm snow, it is even more helpful if the aim is to achieve a high edge angle without any lateral slide. As anyone who observes their fellow man on the slopes can attest, there is more than one way to tip a ski on edge, but there aren't a lot of good ways to get it on edge at the very top of the turn, so that between the two skis that form your carving foundation, you never leave contact with the snow. Getting to the uphill ski's edge early sets the tone for the rest of the turn. It requires commitment and sensitivity and some comfort with speed. The return on this investment is total security on edge, allowing the pilot to set his or her line according to the degree of edge angle applied, feathering the arc without smearing it, the way Vermeer manipulated his brush when simulating the sheen of a pearl.

When you're motoring along at 40mph, every turn may contain an element of surprise. Like presents on Christmas, you don't know what you're going to find at the bottom of the turn until you remove the wrapping at the top. If you set the edge early, you always get the present you want. For a lesson in being early, head off the top of Hidden Peak down the Path to Paradise, which feeds into Mineral Basin. The smooth acceleration of the cat-track gradually builds the energy you will momentarily unleash into White Diamonds

Downhill. As you pass the gun mounted along the edge of the traverse's only tight corner, White Diamonds Downhill will be your next left, groomed ballroom smooth top to bottom, but with an abrupt transition that can only be cannily managed by being early.

As you crest the run, roll your uphill ski on edge and tip your upper body into the fall line. Stand hard on the ski to resist the sudden surge in force generated by the slope's steep pitch, but don't stand on it long. At the peak of the load, step to your uphill ski; the move to the new ski is inseparable from the step off the old, as integrated and uncomplicated as walking. The commitment to the uphill ski is accompanied by leaning the upper body down the pitch, ahead of your skis. It's at the top of the turn, when one has the sense of falling into it, that you can feel the flow of the hill, inviting you to mesh your movements with it. As you move early to the uphill ski it becomes the platform from which you direct the rest of you into the flow. The ski will load naturally as you shift weight and pressure to it, storing the power that will shoot you out the bottom of the arc and into the next. Step, tip, load and release. The more force applied when loading the ski, the lighter the feeling when the load is released. The pressure and release feels like an organic pulse, as natural and rhythmic as breathing.

As the pitch starts to transition into a giant, roundhouse left, you let your ponies run, adding an extra dollop of speed to pull a few more fractions of g force through the compression, luxuriating in the belly of an elongated arc. As you round the corner, you confront a slope that falls sharply away to your right, another opportunity to set up early so when you hit the crest you are already in the heart of your first turn. This pitch transitions into the immense rollers that dominate the bottom of this side of Mineral Basin. Here the instinct for being early translates into matching the roll of the hill with your roll onto the edge, always striving to make that moment come as early as possible. More than a matter of mere mechanics, being early is a mindset, a willingness to seek the cadence of the mountain, a recognition that gravity's stream is always running, and the comprehension that once we visualize its flow it's our sacred duty to enter it.

The view of Mineral Basin from the top of White Diamonds

Chamonix Chutes, Mineral Basin

The hike to High Baldy passes along the top of the Chamonix Chutes

Photographer: Eric Hostetler

Chapter 6

On Altitude

No matter where you go, there you are. This is the primordial flaw in the vacation concept. The principal goal, to get away from oneself, isn't normally achievable. In the era of ubiquitous email, it often isn't even possible to get away from work. Even if you do make it all the way to Bora Bora, while you'll probably return with a tan, you may not feel much change underneath it.

That's because there's more to getting away than just leaving wherever you are. Escaping yourself requires an intense commitment to the moment, an all-in mentality that leaves as little room for doubt as it does for self-consciousness. To find your perfect center in a snowbound world without coordinates requires you move off-center from the everyday person who operates your being. The judgmental entity who nags us from the inside out has to sit down and stick a sock in its maw to allow your centered self to emerge and ride the invisible flow.

This world of self-discovery doesn't exist everywhere or else our lives would be much more interesting, but it exists at high altitude in winter. The top of big mountains are formidable environments, lashed by winds that will remove facial hair and snow that seems to fall in every direction at once. Without ski lifts, only a handful of people might ever ascend to this height. Before lifts, the only people around here were miners who prayed the damn snow would hurry up and melt so they could get back to business. Anyone of that era who would venture to the top while it was under assault by snowstorms would probably not survive the experience.

It's our great good fortune to be alive, not just in this particular place, but in a time when skiing as we know it is possible. As recently as a hundred years ago, mankind didn't see mountains in winter as recreational opportunities but as venues where an already challenging existence turned into a battle for survival. If we weren't living in this time, we would have no means to appreciate this place.

What a gift it is to arrive at the top of Hidden Peak equipped to meet its extraordinary opportunities and engage in such delicious madness. The smog-choked valley below is a harmless metaphor for the life you left behind, the details far too small to matter. Some of the silver the miners sought still lies in undiscovered veins beneath your feet, but the lucre of the past can't compare to the essence of today, two feet of Wasatch white, more precious than any metal, for in its embrace you can find the dance of life.

Unlike the miners who staked successful claims, we skiers produce nothing with a market value. Our medium of exchange is pure ephemera, for it is the ever-vanishing moment when we become indistinguishable from our actions, when we *are* the turn. We find our treasure in the stillness of now. That is our reward, our seam of ore.

To unearth the intangible value in the interaction of gravity, snow and human intent, try doing the dance in the chaos of sightlessness. When the tram operator omits Mineral Basin from the list of closed areas, almost everyone will bolt for the familiar comforts of Powder Paradise or other lines to skier's right. That's when you meander towards the top of Chip's, veer off as if you were going to climb up Baldy then, just as the hill ahead begins to arc upwards, you slip skier's right and find the powder-choked, storm-day blind plunges that are the Chamonix Chutes.

The first couple of entries are steeper at the top and so appear more menacing, but all the lines here are in fact benign the instant you settle into a rhythm. The uninitiated might wonder how to divine a rhythm in a sensory void; converts know rhythm is all you've got. Not seeing is no excuse for not sensing. Maybe you can't see the pitch but you can feel it. Your skis are sinking or floating in accordance with what they encounter; they can be trusted if you trust in them. When they rise, you rise, and unfailingly commit to the void as if you were engaged in a trust exercise with the mountain and gravity. If I drop in the turn, will momentum catch me? Let the splash of snow on weatherproof fabric be your answer. Keep the splashes coming in metered beats and don't forget to breathe.

In the rarified air of big mountains, you depend on a different kind of judgment. You have no data to guide you, no spreadsheets or analytics to inform decision-making. You have to embrace the perfection of the adverse, find direction in the chaos and do it without much more than the will to find the next turn. You can't stop, for that will only exacerbate the sense of isolation and dislocation in a world that no longer seems to rotate on a single axis. Wise skiers prevail by projecting just the smallest degree into the future. They have confidence in a line they cannot see, knowledge of a path that feels behind them before it's here.

It takes a higher mind to find a higher line. No, we're not talking about *that* kind of high; we mean the higher consciousness of high altitude, this strange, separate place that we would never inhabit were it not for our peculiar addiction to self-realization on skis. Here in this separate world we can find our separate selves, the person divorced from the contorted identities of the workplace and family roles. When nature drops a veil of invisibility over a slope like the Chamonix Chutes, we confront a universe of one, with only the compelling hand of gravity to guide us. We become stripped to the essentials of identity, sensation and energy: we are only what we feel this pinprick instant in an ever-shifting flow through different densities of snow. If we don't make turns there are no turns and so we make them, splash, splash, splash.

In flat light it's impossible to say when, but in twenty turns or so you'll reach a transition that levels out. Stay skier's right and after the flats follow the rolling terrain into some scattered trees. This will lead to some low-risk cliff bands with ample lines between them for finding pockets of true love. There's a road below you, Lupine Loop, which you won't see in a whiteout, so keep one foot on the brakes.

If the sun were out, you'd be in sight of two lifts, Baldy Express along the road to skier's right, or Mineral Basin Express more or less directly below. To get here, you carved a path through a maze that wasn't there, found down when it wasn't a self-evident direction, moved using energy the hill let you borrow. When you couldn't see with your eyes, a higher mind nurtured by rare air found a line and with it the confidence to sculpt it in the next, invisible moment.

You're Alice returning from Wonderland, Einstein fresh from bending time; where you've been will forever inform where you go next. You've found a place you've never been, inside you all along.

This is what you return with from the Chamonix Chutes that you can't bring home from Bimini: a person you weren't when you left. The old you, good and bad, will still be there; but so will the soul who found new trust in all that is on the sightless slopes above Mineral Basin.

Chamonix Chutes from below with the first shot groomed

Macaroni Chute to Silver Fox
Thunder Bowl

Entry to Macaroni Chute, Peruvian Gulch

Chapter 7

On Taking What the Mountain Gives You
Or
The Many Shades of Perfect

Americans tend to treat all athletic endeavors as metaphors for war. Our most cherished spectator sports are either grounded in a military ethos (football) or are brutally confrontational (NASCAR, cage fighting) and this winner-moves-on, loser-goes-home mentality bleeds into other arenas. Skiers also compete head-to-head in countless ways (remember ballet?), but 99% of skiers aren't competing for anything yet they often bring to the slopes an attitude that this heart-pounding activity must be a contest with… something.

It's hard to conceive of a less constructive attitude to bring to the mountain. Skiing need not be a battle against others and it must not be a duel with the mountain itself. It's not about winning and it's certainly not about beating someone. Thanks to advanced GPS technology, it's now possible to track every moment of your ski day, including your top speed, vertical consumed, number of runs, steepest pitch, every stat you can dream up; it's not about that, either.

Skiing is about discovering something about yourself that you wouldn't otherwise learn. It's about getting off the groomers and following the path into the trees. It's about challenging your assumptions about what constitutes perfection. There are some skiers who will only eat powder; others who dine only on groomage. Both are missing the point of why we ski in the first place. The path to self-discovery is not measured in the number of consecutive blue trams caught or the depth of the powder plumbed that day. To find what you're really looking for requires a different relationship with the mountain, not an adversarial one, but a bond, a connection via passion, understanding, respect, and yes, love.

It's not about making turns. You can make turns on any mountain; that's what redeems the smaller hills skiers often grow up on. It's where we learn the discipline of cutting edges into a surface that fights back, a skill that transfers to any alpine environment. But once the training wheels come off and it's time to discover the treasures that only big mountains can hide, you learn to match your turns to the mountain as you find it. There is no one way to ski the mountain because the mountain is never the same. The pre-Socratic philosopher Heraclitus said you can't cross the same river twice. The same could be said of big mountains in winter.

And, heresy of heresy in Little Cottonwood Canyon, it's not about feasting on powder. Those who only ski on powder days will never know the epiphany of consistently creasing wind-deposit lines or revel in the tantalizing skill of navigating wind slab, to say nothing of the quotidian pleasures of corn and corduroy. Without their 40 inches of 8% (water content) powder they can't adjust to a world, however temporary, of 40 inches of 0%. Their eyes don't see this other shade of perfection in part because they don't know where to look but more importantly because they haven't learned how to look. The trick is to take what the mountain gives you and in that gift, to find your reward.

As Olivia Newton-John once sang, let's get physical. Suppose it's a blustery day, a wild wind tearing out of the south in sidelong swirls that skitter across the snow surface, obscuring all objects more than ten yards away. The snow seems in a panic to be someplace else, yet even snow driven by winds both fierce and fickle has to land somewhere, and that somewhere is often Macaroni Chute, a tight, steep, north-facing shot some five to tens turns long. You can check it out from the tram as it approaches Tower 4, to scout the quality of the wind-buff that loads in between the rock cliffs that define the chute's boundaries.

The easiest way to gain entry to the goods is the gate at Tower 4. Once you are in the slot, keep your speed in check as the exit is guarded by dramatic shark fins of rock that will put a real dent in your day if you clip one. A hard left past the exit sends you towards the even steeper North Chute, while straight below lie the cliff features of Silver Fox and Rock Chute. If you traverse left out of Rock Chute you will find other pockets where the south wind will have left a present of uncut cream. Alternatively, if you head skier's right out of Macaroni you'll be poised to hit Primrose Path. On the upper slope, aim for the scattered tree features to provide some reference in flat light, then hew to the right tree line for better visibility through the lower gully and on into Chip's flats.

When the wind is transporting snow to Macaroni and the slopes immediately below it, you can lap run after run and never cross your own tracks. These are the true powder days, with perfection on demand for as long as your legs hold you up. You never experience that on a bluebird pow day, when all is ravaged in an hour. By taking what the mountain gives you, you discover other shades of perfection.

Skiing the mountain as you find it means you can't always cling to familiar routes. Some skiers treat the tram as the mother ship, literally; they get separation anxiety if their run doesn't conclude in the plaza. The problem with tram dependency is it limits one's options when conditions are at their best along the resort's boundaries. One of those boundaries resides looker's right off the Gad 2 chair, through the first gate at the top of Bananas, past a short uphill bump that requires 2 minutes of sidestepping before the trail catches a gradual traverse that delivers you to the gate for Thunder Bowl. As you stand at this threshold, the trail falling off to your right is Tiger Tail, a worthy descent in its own right. After passing the "Open" sign, the first shot on your right highlights low shrubberies dotting succulent steeps. The next drop-in is more open at the top, with larger trees to play through, but tightens like a python's coil as you get lower. Subsequent lines are ever more open, which creates more sun exposure, so keep that in mind when choosing your line.

The lower half of Thunder Bowl has two distinct features: to skier's right is a large timbered area, which drops off at an extremely steep pitch (over 45°) littered with rock outcroppings, short stubby trees, and little rhythm to speak of; to skier's left, directly down the fall line, is Exit Gully, which in a good snow year offers an open glade of coniferous delight. Thunder Bowl was a less popular destination before Exit Gully was cleared of trees by an avalanche that deposited the lumber against the top of Baby Thunder lift. Below this naturally cleared path is a steep section that breaks into two distinct fall lines that converge into a tight gully that drops you at the top of the Baby Thunder Chair. If that chair isn't running, don't ski any lower than the last traverse to the Gadzoom lift, or you'll be walking.

One of the adventures available off the Thunder Bowl traverse is continuing through the backcountry gate, which leads around to Scottie's Bowl. This bit of exploration presents some return access issues, so plan ahead before you tackle it. If the backcountry gate is closed, don't cross it. Gate violations close access to Thunder Bowl for everybody, so please respect the patrol and your fellow seekers by respecting closed boundaries.

One reason we devote so much of our lives to skiing is that catching lines like Macaroni and Thunder Bowl isn't like other forms of exercise. It's not like going for a run, working out at the gym, or playing golf or tennis, if for no other reason than you can't do any of these other activities while rocketing along at 40 mph down a steeply sloped forest. There's curative, rejuvenating magic in finding the calm center of your own energy field, feeling as if the world is racing past while you dance in a single place that keeps on changing.

Thunder Bowl

Baldy Traverse, the eastern border of Peruvian Gulch. Once upon a time, the High Baldy area was permanently closed, and a close look at the lines through the cliff bands and evergreen glades of this rugged acreage reveals why. While there are a few ways down wide enough to be considered tame, many of the shots here are on the wild side.

To access the High Baldy Traverse, head off the tram down the Chips Access Road, but instead of dropping skier's left into Chips, go straight across the flat ridge that separates Mineral Basin from Peruvian Gulch. When the hill rises in front of you, pop off your skis and hike up for a few minutes and you'll soon be standing on the traverse. To properly reward your effort, pass up the first few faces you see as these lines bottom out rather quickly. Right after wrapping around an exposed shoulder, look to your left and when you see an encouraging opening, take it.

The Cirque Traverse marks the eastern edge of Gad Valley; its western flank is accessed from the top of Hidden Peak via the Road to Provo. This wide-open cat-track offers unobstructed views of the terrain ahead and instant access to the playground of Little Cloud bowl. If you stay on this lateral route past Mark Malu, you'll have the choice of upper and lower gates leading to Pipeline Bowl, the Rasta Chutes, Last Choice and the Knucklehead Traverse, which continues the cross-hill trek to the top of the Gad 2 lift. If your left leg hasn't permanently shortened by now, you can extend the sideward sashay all the way through the Tiger Tail gate and onward to the resort's western boundary.

The traverse that etches the upper edge of Mineral Basin is the Path to Paradise, which segues into the Bookends Traverse, leading to the Bookends and the Sunday Cliffs. This is mostly exposed terrain, easily scoped from the Mineral Basin Express. A rich variety of pitches are vulnerable to attack from all along this elongated, semi-circular crescent. To expedite your cross-country trek, employ this age-old traversing trick: as you lift your uphill leg, angle your heel outward and toe-in the tip of your ski so when you set it down again the ski is angled slightly downhill. When you move your weight to this ski, it will glide forward slightly, adding propulsion to a step that would otherwise have been neutral at best. You'll cut your traversing time and effort in half.

These are the major traverses that define the perimeter of each of the mountain's central amphitheaters, but the lower mountain is likewise crisscrossed with traverses, some of which are main arteries, some of which are thread-thin capillaries, but all of which cross someone's idea of a downhill run. And herein lies a conundrum.

When the traversing skier is downhill of another skier or rider who is attacking the fall line, both can lay claim to the right of way. By convention, the uphill skier is responsible for the downhill skier's protection, but the downhill skier is also entitled to stay in the flow of the fall line, which the traversing skier should respect. Our empathy is with the skier who is already engaged with the hill, as the skier below him has the obligation to look uphill as he crosses traffic. If you were about to cross a road, wouldn't you look to see if the coast were clear? Yes, the downhill, traversing skier has the right to safe passage across the fall line, but rights don't avoid accidents, vigilance does. When on any mid-slope traverse, especially underneath ultra steep, tight, and blind lines, it's imperative to keep an eye uphill along the way. If the traverse passes under cliff bands, remember every rock is someone's idea of a drop zone, so keep it moving and head to open space as expeditiously as possible. Please remember we're all riding the vortex together, so keep an eye out for one another and share the road responsibly.

Any prolonged slash across the hill qualifies as a traverse, and with all the open terrain at Snowbird it's possible to create one's own traverse almost anywhere. Cutting across several lanes to find better snow is a time-honored tactic, but any extended lateral moves should be preceded by an over-the-shoulder inspection of the uphill traffic situation. For every traverser still seeking the perfect line, there's a fall-line skier already immersed in it. If each can acknowledge that at some other time the roles were reversed, both should be able to ride gravity's stream with the confidence that for this ride, at this time, two bodies won't attempt to occupy the same space at the same time.

The Road to Provo

Anderson's Hill

Getting ready to let go at the bottom of Anderson's Hill

Chapter 10

On Trust

All our lives we depend on others. It's implicit in infancy, unavoidable in adolescence, negotiated in marriage and fundamental to friendship. As long as we live, we will be dependent on oxygen and have to trust that, with or without string theory, in *our* universe gravity will continue to tether us to the planet. So there are things we trust with our lives already, we just assume them and so don't count them. When we trust our lives on skis, however, somehow the consequences seem so much more tangible. Less abstract, more painful. And so very, very dependent on us alone.

That's the big question, isn't it? Not can you trust your skis, or the laws of nature or your cousin the CPA, but can you trust yourself? When the you-know-what hits the F-A-N, who do you trust to skipper your ship to safe harbor? Is there anyone on board who knows what to do in a crisis?

We hope you didn't say, "My conscious mind." That cowboy is as useless as gills on a buzzard. Whenever disaster impends, your conscious mind has no time to call a committee to order, review the

agenda, evaluate strengths and weaknesses and decide what you're
going to do to live through the next microsecond. An automatic
response is all you have to depend on, and if it doesn't happen NOW,
you're toast.

The response you summon is whatever your body has been
trained to believe. While you can't train your body for every
contingency, you don't have to. It has a remarkable instinct for self-
preservation. When you stumble stepping off the sidewalk, it knows
to shuffle the loose foot forward ASAP. You don't have to think and
it wouldn't have helped if you had, for you would've been nose-to-
asphalt before you summarized the situation. Instead, you trusted an
automatic response and it came through before you could even
consciously call for its intervention. That's the guy (or gal) you want
making the snap-quick judgments that avert disaster and keep you
out of tomorrow's headlines.

If you want autopilot to save you, you need to practice skiing
without thinking about skiing. You need to trust your body to get the
job done unsupervised. Which is not to say that thoughts have no
influence on your body; the problem is your mind has *a lot* of
influence on your body, more than enough to screw it up completely.
If you complicate the skiing process with a litany of internal chatter
your chances of skiing well approach zero. Instead of some silly bit
of instruction filling the space between your ears, focus the mind on
the path ahead and let the body draw from a well of perfect images
and feelings to choose the right action at the right moment.

The conscious mind is terribly clever, but its ability to construct
and communicate the commands necessary to function through

moguls at 30 miles per hour, or in any terrain when topping 60 mph, is impaired. Skiing makes it possible to travel too fast to think; instead, you learn to travel at the speed of trust. At the velocities World Cup racers swoosh downhill they have to be able to visualize their entire run, almost as if it were a single thought. If visualization can achieve total clarity, if the movie in your mind runs in HD without skipping a frame, your body can draw on this image as if it were a behavior map and simulate the motions imprinted in the imagination.

To achieve that super-sharp image of the perfect turn, practice seeing it and feeling it in your mind's eye. This is immensely easier to do once one has already done it, and frightfully difficult to do if one hasn't, but the quickest way to acquire skills is still to see them first. The next trick is to internalize what you see so intensely that you can feel the motion, the build-up of pressure under the foot as the ski loads, followed by the ineluctable moment of early commitment to the uphill ski as you steer into the top of the turn. Once you can see it and feel it, you can do it. Just remember to shut down your thinking, judging self before takeoff, so your body has a chance to draw on your image library without interference.

Getting your judging self to shut the hell up can be quite the obstacle. In social circles this is often achieved with alcohol, but this is a very bad idea as a ski learning method. There are two things you can do on every run that will keep the onboard hectoring at bay. First, create a trigger mechanism, one you instantly obey, which is your signal to end all self-talk. This can be a quick lift of the goggles off the face, a click of the poles together, a stomp of the feet, any simple, repeatable act that invariably and immediately precedes takeoff. The message of this act is always the same: it's time to turn off the computer, focus on the hill ahead and go skiing.

This may work brilliantly until you make your first bobble, your first slump back into an old, vile habit. Instantly your internal Judge Judy renders an unfavorable ruling, citing your history of failure and rattling your confidence. But there is a way to muzzle her, and that's the second trick: put some music on in your head, either piped in off your iPod or sourced from memory, and play it loud. Let the music occupy all the space in your head and there will be no place for a self-judge to sit. The judge may as well get up and join the dance because there will be no more judging now.

So sharpen the focus on your in-flight movie, put your music on, hit your trigger and trust your body's ability to imitate the perfect image in your mind. When you ski well, you are your movements. You are unmediated sensation, feeling both in the flow and of it, blurring the barrier between yourself and the medium you move through, until you are so aware, you're gone.

You can't get to this transcendental state without letting go, which is the embodiment of trust. Letting go can mean straight-running Anderson's Hill from the top, or laying your hips so far over on the last pitch of Regulator Johnson you can feel the G's flowing through your body like electricity. Letting go might happen in the bumps under Peruvian, where you find the pattern in the chaos, pouring down battle-scarred bumps like mercury, adding the syncopation of air just because there is beauty in flight. Letting go is an immersion into confidence, a celebration of the security of skill, the awareness that you have judged the exit from North Chute in tempo with your turns so you can admire and appreciate the rock you pass rather than fear it.

If we're letting go, acting on autopilot and sending our reasoning selves to go sit in the corner and mind their own business, just what is the apparatus on our shoulders up to whilst we rocket down the hill? Our personal prayer is that it's watching where the show is heading and anticipating where, in the looming maze of trails, terrain features and fellow citizens, to go next. Safety first. Who else is on the radar, and at what speed are they closing? Are there any one-eyed skiers, aka snowboarders, who have no clue you are sharing the same slope and trajectory? Are there any of the less fortunate stemming their way trepidatiously downhill, to whom we owe the courtesy of a wide berth? If we're skiing with any buddies, have we allowed room for them in our calculations? Oh, there are many and splendid things to occupy the mind while we hurtle through space and time, but how to make a turn need not and ought not to be one of them.

Trust is the doorway to salvation, the ideology of success. Like anticipation, trust looks forward to that which not yet is and does more than just envisions it, it believes in it. Trust combines energy, imagery and will to create an improbable outcome that might have 1,000 iterations in other worlds, but not in this one, not in this time, where everything is perfect.

Sunday Cliffs, Mineral Basin

Roundness is all. The sun over Snowbird.

Chapter 11

On Roundness

In the White World of the mountains, every line is a curve. The innocents who proudly announce that they straight-lined such-and-such a slope failed to observe that every inch of their descent described an arc through space. (Through time as well, but let's not complicate matters any further for now.) Once atop a mountain, the instant you step into gravity's stream you go from standing on a dot to standing on a curve. The awareness that you move in a universe defined by curvature should influence your movements. As you respond to the rhythm of roundness that is the pulse of the mountain, you become the curvature you create. Being and doing dissolve into one another when you occupy the still center of the curve.

Once you learn to balance in the center of the arc, your mind no longer needs to fret about line or trajectory or edge angle as all are determined below the level of consciousness. Now your mental mischief-maker can absorb the advantages of the mountain's rare air, a clarity it won't find in the un-White World, a refreshing absence of clutter, a filter over the static that normally preoccupies the mind. The air at 8,000 feet isn't thin, it's rich, it's the elixir, the invisible tonic that drops scales from the eyes and unchains shackles from possibility.

We would add that the air is also free, but it's not. Yes, it's just air and you won't get a bill for it, but you will have to earn it. The air alone won't free a preoccupied mind that is buzzing with the everyday interference that keeps us from accessing our best selves. It has to enter more than just your lungs; it has to infuse all of you, and for that to happen you must disappear into the moment where doing and being meld.

To pass through the portal where roundness hangs its hat, you have to leave your baggage behind. Remember the primacy of the idea: as long as you think about something you draw power to it, just as it pulls power from you. But your mind can't be in two places at once when you really need it to be no place at all. All distractions need to be dumped in a sealed compartment so the blank mind can focus on the path ahead. Your body will perform amazing feats if given a chance, but it has no chance if you aren't centered, calm and, in a way, empty-minded. When you're the calm center, you'll have all the time and space you need to stay round.

The antipode to roundness is the right angle, the square, the grid; all iconic shapes of the un-White World. We have to leave the world of boxes behind if we are to step into the natural, cyclic flow of the White World, where gravity's stream roars silently. In the White World, the inflexible formality of the square is replaced with the ineffable fractals -the indefinable edges - of trees and snowflakes. You are in the world of curvature.

Roundness is never rounder than when it's a funnel, the continuous swirl we ride as we carve down the mountain. The swirl is Yin and Yang in motion, a vortex that echoes every significant cycle in nature, from the growth pattern of leaves to the emanations of light itself. When water vapor refracting in the air allows us to see the energy streaming from the sun, the image that we see is a circle, the indivisible, geometric manifestation of light's perfection. The rainbow also serves to remind us that light follows the path of the vortex, the turn without end.

Wherever we are on the mountain, whenever we step into gravity's stream, we open a portal into the continuous flow of the vortex. The motions of galaxies, hurricanes and whirlpools obey the same mathematics that we engage when we join the stream, following where the current leads. To truly become part of a stream, you, too, must be liquid; then you and the cadence of the mountain will be one. Its power will be yours, the power of feeling an incorruptible connection with the vortex, of being not just *in* the flow, like a rock in the stream, but *of* the flow, a minute section of the larger circle.

Stepping into the flow doesn't mean you must descend with the acceleration of a particle in a cyclotron. To manage speed while still finding the flow, change your frequency to a faster beat, tighten your wavelength until you again attain equilibrium with the current. You'll know you're there when the sensation of gravity disappears and you become inseparable from the stream. Like a small craft in a powerful river, the shore flies by, but in relation to the rushing water, you're still.

When we float silently in the stream, we move with its rhythm, following the geometry of the mountain. As students of cymatics know, geometry and music are intrinsically bound: every elemental structure in nature knows its own note, just as all notes *are* the shapes they generate. When we ski, with each curve we cut, we make a note; with each run, a musical passage. We become the crystals that seek and find the shape of a particular vibration.

To make music, a fiddler needs a violin, and a skier needs a ski. A ski is a remarkable instrument, created with its own innate sense of curvature. The ski's contribution to a carved turn – locked within its sidecut - can only be released by the skier's application of edge angle on one axis and sufficient pressure to bend the ski along a perpendicular axis. The resulting turn shape can be altered within the more-than-sufficient 0-to-90 degree range of ski edge angle to the snow available to the skier. If you know your ski, you should be able to make any kind of music you want.

To coin a fresh oxymoron, the point of roundness is the more complete the arc, the more the ski sings. By holding onto the curvature, loading the ski up with pressure in the belly of the turn redirects lateral forces and drives your boards forward on an unwavering arc. Try not to blur the notes: don't let gravity's force leak to the side but stick it on the line, the pure note of your trajectory. When you bury the ski in the belly of the turn, you load the arrow, filling the ski with the energy to rip the bottom of the turn and carry you effortlessly into the next.

We ride a curved tool on a curved slope as part of a larger cycle that feeds us to the top of the gravity stream so we can ride it down, in essence filling our gravity account with every ascent and draining it with every splurge downhill. To find our favorite forms of gravity-fed roundness we often resort to those shallow curves we call traverses, and so we shall, as we head off to Mineral Basin and the Sunday Cliffs.

As you travel along the Path to Paradise, maintain your momentum and keep an eye out to your right just after you pass the first entry to White Diamonds. A sudden, upwards diagonal track marks the start of the Bookends Traverse, which you will follow all the way to the short uphill jag known as the Hillary Step. Now you're looking into The Bookends, which sounds like the end of the trail, but just beyond lies the sweet, low-angle pitch of the Sunday Cliffs where, after a northwest storm has deposited a 10-inch blanket of fluffulescence, roundness resides.

Before you push off, align your skis with the fall line, sticking your tails in the snow behind you to hold you in place in gravity's stream. Feel the cadence of the hill ahead and let it infuse you. See yourself at the bottom; time travel a few moments ahead to when you *are* roundness, your self synonymous with your trajectory. See roundness informed by flow in your mind, hit your trigger and go.

To instantly find your roundness, maintain a quiet core, the center of a pendulum that swings your feet side to side. You'll know your inner metronome is connected to the mountain when time expands, when the moment becomes elastic and you disappear into the spaces between notes. There is no turn to fight, for you are the turn, its geometry and its music. While there is an effort tax for achieving such transcendence, it's minimal compared to the tariff for fighting the flow.

The only demerits to a descent down Sunday Cliffs are that the pitch declines too soon, and if you chase the last ounce of energy you'll be looking up at your only way out. So we advise that you milk each moment, elongate the present, luxuriate in the life force you were somehow blessed to receive. The vanity of ego evaporates as feeling supplants thinking in the wheelhouse that governs intent. All thought of skiing itself, any chattering, internal babble about mechanics, are muffled by the ecstasy of a moment that stretches far enough to touch the eternal.

In the silence of the White World, you can hear the call of your inner voice. Presence in the moment provides the sanctuary where being can hear a chord of purpose that was struck at birth and perhaps not heard since. When you join the flow on the Sunday Cliffs, you'll discover that with awareness comes joy. Indeed, every time you open the door to gravity's stream, you have a fresh opportunity to find the cadence of the hill, to re-create while you recreate, to match action and transcendence in an energy field where the shortest distance between two points is a curve.

High Baldy Traverse to Fields of Glory

Fields of Glory, High Baldy

Chapter 12

On Hands and Feet

Let's be clear on one point from the get-go: you don't ski with your hands. Your hands are über-important, as we're about to relate, but they're not feet. If we skied with our hands, we'd have little skis on them instead of mittens or gloves. Since skis are instead on our feet, feet become the primordial appendage, but hands are a close second. The two tandem players ought to operate in unison, just as they do when you stride. Of all the activities to which skiing can be compared, the one that most closely resembles it is walking. It's just that you're able to walk very, very fast.

Because the feet are doing the heavy lifting, there are all sorts of things the hands can be doing while you ski along, as anyone observing on-slope behavior can attest. There's the ex-racer who still hallucinates gates, knocking imaginary slalom poles out of the way with every direction change, his hands busier than if he were swatting away a swarm of bees. There's Mr. Double Pole-Plant, firing both barrels ahead, accompanying each forward thrust of the upper body with a disconnected wiggle of the hips. Robot Mom holds both her hands in the upright and locked position from which they never move. Lord only knows what the monoskiers are up to. The trench digger lays over every turn as if he were channeling Ted Ligity; there's barely enough room for a fist under his laid-over legs, much less a ski pole, which instead is tucked out of the way in his slipstream. The mogul meister may ski with a pole cut short enough for a midget, and pipe and park rats use poles so stumpy we should have another name for them, like pipettes.

Despite this diversity, each of these citizens manages to get down the hill, albeit with mixed success and varying degrees of aesthetic appeal. The unifying thread that runs through all of these techniques isn't biomechanical, but psychological: each of them knows, from the frozen haus-frau to the imaginary gate-basher, that their hands are important. They do what they do because they understand that, as goes their manual units, so goes the union of their hurtling bodies. Every element that makes up the entirety of the skier is linked to every other, but nowhere is the bond greater than between hands and feet.

The primal importance of hand position is never more evident than when your feet fail you. Suppose you're picking your way down the moguls that dot the top of Silver Fox when the downhill skips out and your hips rotate out of the fall line; you're heading for a rag-doll, pinwheel adventure with at best a graceless outcome unless, in that same instant, you find your uphill hand and punch it downhill with whatever power you can generate. This headfirst lunge down the fall line will square your shoulders and unlock your hips, giving your skis a chance to cut under you. With hands, shoulders and hips in the fall line, skis cannot be far behind, and just as suddenly as you envisioned certain doom you are back in the saddle.

Even when you're not about to eat it, your hands tell the rest of your body what to do while your feet are busy making turns. Your torso is attuned to your hands' bossy attitude; it will always try to follow their lead. So keep them forward, point them where you want to go and don't get lazy with the uphill hand. Generations of skiers have been taught to plant the pole on the inside of the turn, so that hand often is extended, as if in greeting, to the fall line, while the uphill hand takes a nap somewhere alongside the thigh. Until you are a skier of world-class capabilities, you cannot afford sleepy hands. The uphill hand that you've left in a mini-coma will be called upon in a trice to reach again downhill; it should be in an on-call position, not on sabbatical. It should be carried no lower than it would be if you were about to draw a sidearm from a holster. You're engaged in an athletic endeavor, so try to look like it.

Like an orchestra conductor, a skier can use his or her hands to add emphasis to a given beat. To get extra drive on the downhill ski when you have to hold an arc at speed, press the hand above that ski down over it, as if it were exerting a force field down on the ski's nervous forebody, and use the bonus force to push off the edge and transition to the uphill ski. It may sound more like telekinesis than Newtonian physics, but the hands inform the feet all the way down the mountain.

Watch as coaches or talented instructors try to explain how to pressure and edge a ski; inevitably they will demonstrate foot position using their hands. Holding their palms down and fingers extended, they bank their hands side to side, simulating the foot positions that define the most accurate, efficient edging technique. Look at those hand movements and think of your feet moving your boots on parallel planes. Let your mind absorb the concept: turning is about edge angles; edge angles are about tilting your boot soles; tilting your boots can be effected with ankle, knee and/or hip; and seamless transitions between turns are about changing edge angle and pressure in harmony with the hill.

The interdependence of hands and feet, while always in play, is perhaps most in evidence when skiing deep powder. The hands are up and out of the snow, helping to keep the upper body erect and balanced. They hold the keys to quietude, a message to the trunk to keep cool, calm and collected so the feet can do their business unimpeded. And the feet are busy indeed, busier than the hands, which only have to keep the beat while the feet switch angles nearly every instant. Invisible beneath the churn of flying snow, your feet increase their banking angle as the legs extend them to the side, then gradually reduce it to zero at the moment they pass under your butt before replicating the variable banking motion in the other direction. Your feet would have a hell of a time doing this efficiently if your hands weren't helping to keep your core in neutral.

But even brilliant feet working in synchronicity with properly positioned hands can't do everything. They need the cooperation of one other partner in particular: your head. At the risk of stating the obvious, your head should be engaged in the business of figuring out where you're going. This seemingly simple-minded advice is pertinent because most skiers do this rather poorly. If they were driving a car instead of skiing, they would be looking no further ahead than the hood ornament. This is why events sometimes overtake skiers first learning to attack the fall line; they don't look far enough ahead to anticipate terrain that will be under them in a heartbeat. The further you can learn to look down the hill, the more clearly you can envision your immediate future. Then your skiing can evolve from the mechanics of turning to flowing, to moving with the hill in a dynamic dance in which you are the ever-changing, ever-quiet center.

The acid test for coordinating hands and feet is managing speed on steeps, particularly those precipitous lines that narrow to a dicey choke point requiring a well-timed exit. This is a fair description of many of the lines that spill off High Baldy, so let's steer our pedal extremities in that direction.

You know this cliff-striped adventure park is in play when the tram concierge omits High Baldy from the litany of area closures announced just before docking at the top of Hidden Peak. Try not to betray your excitement, for only a few cognoscenti will have grasped the significance of this non-utterance, and like any great powder field, High Baldy is best when savored first. To catch the High Baldy Traverse, toddle as inconspicuously as you can straight past the top of Chips, hewing to the ridgeline, and when the hill begins to rise in front of you, start climbing.

If one is fit, it only takes about 6 minutes to climb up to where the traverse begins, and if you're not fit you'll find a well-packed trail to follow. As you climb, reflect on the fact that Baldy was for many years a permanently closed area; in a few more minutes you'll discover why. Endorphins will start to flow in anticipation of the Big Boom Bah that lies ahead. Your awareness of your wild, other-world surroundings sharpens. As soon as your skis are back on, you'll be hyped to snatch the first yummy goods you see, but you'll forfeit some vertical by not moving on, so onward you go, traversing around a sharp corner that comes up fairly quickly. The wind batters this exposed crease in the mountain, so you take the lower line to avoid the variable conditions of the high line. Just ahead, a playground of infinite permutations awaits, with big lines off to skier's right or, sliding over further, ultra-steep veins against the cliff. Still further on, the Comma Chutes are a good call, but if you are one of the few who arrive here first, Fields of Glory beckons just below you, sitting, waiting, pristine.

Because of your perspicacity you have a one-tram lead on the general public, giving you time to stick your tails in the snow so your skis aim straight down the gravity stream. The current runs fast on Baldy, so as you lean into it you must commit to its flow, finding the inner cadence to match it, allowing you to stand still in the moment even as you glide with quickening pace downhill. Here is where hands and feet have business to do, the hands setting the beat, the feet guiding the ship. By holding your hands high you remind your upper body to stand tall, for maximum elasticity when required. Your feet probe the snow at varying angles, feeling the resistance build and by that feel knowing when to release the energy you're generating. Your turns form a wave like a tone from a tuning fork, a tone emanating from the mountain, a tone with which you harmonize as you descend in gravity's rhythmic embrace.

Wrapped in a multi-sensory mosaic unlike anything else, profoundly immersed in the moment of now, your conscious attention is focused with full intensity on the glistening terrain ahead. At 30 mph you and the wave are one, but a choke point rushes towards you, so you bring it down, always keeping hands and feet moving in harmony with the hill.

Whenever you move through hairy terrain, remember that what looks perilous to you is mother's milk to many of the denizens of this fabled mountain. It's best to consider every terrain feature a potential launch pad and every other skier a possible astronaut. Most of all, realize that for every launch there is a landing, so don't dawdle in the landing zone. Getting out ahead gets you out of the way and buys you a buffer of tranquility in your pursuit of the perfect line where hands and feet can move in synch with the mountain.

High Baldy looking deceptively benign

Hoopie's Crotch, Gad Valley

Old Ladies

The Goo, neatly stacked

Courtesy of Powder Shots

Chapter 13

On Stacking the Bones

One of the many theories propounded by the young Sherlock Holmes to his new roommate Dr. John Watson was his conviction that the storehouse of memory was not infinite. If Holmes wished to retain an entire catalogue in his head of the various kinds of mud in and around London, he couldn't waste precious storage space on twaddle like astronomy. The body has an analogous problem with muscular energy: there's only so much of it one can expend on a ski day, and when it's gone, it's gone.

Just skiing one run can consume every ounce of energy the human body can generate. Observe how elite athletes on the World Cup circuit occasionally collapse in exhaustion after a run that might not last two minutes. Of course what they are doing bears as little relation to recreational skiing as Formula One does to driving to the 7-11; they're *trying* to expend every erg of energy in their mad dash to the finish line. In contrast, everyday skiers with ambitions of skiing bell to bell had better harbor whatever energy they can muster or they'll need supplemental oxygen by noon. This issue is only exacerbated by the literally tiresome subject of aging: how to conjure up a full day of skiing on reassembled limbs taking instructions from a damaged spine?

There are two ways to marshal the energy to ski from the first early tram to the last ride of the day: train year-round until you have the physical conditioning of a Navy Seal, or learn to stack your bones. Stacking your bones is all about energy conservation, keeping your reserve tank full so you can draw on it as needed. If you stack your bones, you don't have to remain chained to groomers to preserve your fuel; you can take your game anywhere on the mountain and still have glide in your stride when the lifts stop spinning.

Stacking the bones is all about using your skeleton whenever possible so muscular energy can be reserved for special occasions like trenching a few turns or dodging an exposed root or a Citizen Appearing Unexpectedly Standard Emergency (CAUSE), the guy who suddenly drops into the cat-track right in front of you while carefully looking the opposite direction. (Why is it skiers and especially snowboarders exhibit behavior on the slopes that would kill them instantly on the highway? Why do they still roam freely among us? But we digress.) As we were saying, the objective is to save muscular contractions for error correction or propulsive actions meant to solve a particular puzzle that may occur at the bottom of the turn.

So how do you stack your bones? You assume the basic athletic stance, with some ankle flex and knee flex, with hips, torso and shoulders in a uniform plane perpendicular to the line of travel. The upper body projects down the hill, committing to the turn early and calmly. The legs underneath communicate force and pressure in a direct line from the center of body mass in the hips, through a centered knee down to the ball of the foot, and thence to the edge. If the bones are in alignment, muscular effort can be minimized while driving a clean, no-spray edge.

Please note, stacking the bones does not assure *zero* expenditure of effort. Just the slight degree of knee and ankle flex required will put a little tension on the quads. (If this is too taxing, maybe gravity-fed sports aren't for you.) Your upper body should be relaxed, a column at once fluid and unmoving, the epicenter of every movement across the hill. The attitude of your body is one of leaning forward and into the turn, moving just ahead of gravity's stream, your skis cradling the belly of a round arc. Your onboard scanners check for terrain changes and incoming traffic; otherwise, you just keep your column calm, stack your bones directly with your lines of force and feel the pleasure of an arc crafted by speed, edge angle and the application of forces you have only to channel rather than generate.

Getting back to the business of stacking *your* bones, in particular, to do it right you need to know your body and how you stand on your skis when you put the show in motion. Not all stances are created equal. Some people, including most women, have their butt drop behind their heels when they "accordion," or flex at ankles and knees. (This is why women's skis often feature a forward mounting position and women's boots an elevated heel.) From a backseat stance, you will abuse your muscles like they were rental skis in rock season. To stack the bones, the skier must pleat so that the center of mass stays over the center of balance, otherwise known as the feet. If this doesn't happen naturally, whether due to a pear-shaped body, a rigid mid-foot and/or a long femur – all of which will send the hips aft – a ¼-inch heel lift between the inner boot and the shell footbed should tilt your body sufficiently forward to shift your hips over your heels. The heel lift will also have the salubrious effect of shifting weight subtly to the ball of the foot and against the front of the boot, where it belongs.

It's fairly easy to find this stacked position statically. Without bending at the waist, you should be able to sag into this position just by adding some ankle and knee flex. If you were made with a flexible wire core, like a pipe cleaner, your torso would be stick-straight with a slight forward cant, with the thighs angled a bit forward and the calves back. It's the standard athletic "ready position," and it works as well at 60mph as it does at zero.

This position is just as easy to retain dynamically as it is to achieve statically, as long as the pilot is relaxed, in balance, calm and focused on trajectory rather than technique. (Trajectory is even more important in skiing than in golf, for in skiing you're the ball.) Your body will know what to do automatically if you only give it a chance and you start from a centered stance.

By the way, skis, as weight-displacement devices, are very sensitive to position. They do not perform equally well no matter how you stand on them. Some, like most K2's, seem to have a sweet spot the size of Kansas, while others, like Völkl's, will slap you silly if you're off-center. But all of them care where you stand. The current infatuation with multiple stance positions, driven by the switch pipe-and-park crowd, isn't new: ESS bindings were pitching the virtues of 7 different discrete settings back in the 80's. The idea was as inane then as now: sure, a ski behaves differently if you move all over it; so would a car if you moved the wheels back and forth under the frame. That doesn't mean there isn't an *optimal* position from which ski and skier are most likely to remain in blissful balance, which ski makers kindly indicate with a boot midsole mark on the ski.

So, is there more than one great place to stand on a ski? Not if you're aiming downhill without an 180° kink in your spine. So stand where you should, as you should, and life on skis will become a whole lot simpler. Your centered, stacked stance will allow for maximum elasticity, so you can segue from two-dimensional snow to 3D conditions and never miss a beat. Let's take a run from the top and feel how stacking the bones works as we move into different terrain situations. To make it sporting, let's imagine the snow conditions are an amalgam of heinous, semi-set-up powder riven with trenches and topped with a slight zipper crust. Dialing in the roundness in these interference patterns, with or without a moguled undersurface, will oblige you to set a cadence that will carry you through whatever lies ahead.

In this particular example, let's drop into Old Ladies off the Road to Provo. Here, the variable depth, crustiness, and off-on inconsistency will push the ligament stress to near the ripping stage if you aren't careful about when you commit your upper body and attendant bones down the hill. The key on Old Ladies' consistent pitch is to commit to the fall line with surrender. The mental attitude that guides the body is maintaining focus on the *bottom of the hill* – not the next turn, the next instant - but the total trajectory of the run is oriented by focusing on the bottom. In a gravity-fed sport you are always connected to the bottom whether you activate that connection or not.

Focusing your energy towards the bottom of the mountain will pull your solar plexus center quietly into the vortex as you ride the energy stream that constantly runs downhill. This is where stacking the bones comes into play. You want your body aligned over your skis so that you stay centered while the energy in the ski cuts through the snow. You give the ski that energy by standing on it and pressuring it so its forward momentum drives it through the turn on a confident, slashing edge.

Following the slice line set by the ski will let you stand with centered quietude as the turn unfolds. Skiing through the arc lets the tip penetrate terrain and snow variations without deflection. It's this moment of calmness in the turn that allows you to take advantage of the natural release at the point of transition, which, if you are still focused on the bottom, will let you, again, tip into the fall line, and move through snow variations with minimal lateral stress. Working a natural pendulum action will utilize your speed kinetics to blast directly through chop with no deflection and minimal exertion. Don't be afraid to exaggerate that banking attitude of flight as you ride the arrow through the turn, standing at the center of each turn's trajectory.

Even if you don't stack your bones, your body still hoards immense reserves of energy that it holds in abeyance until under mortal threat. It is this unimaginable capacity that allows men to lift boats, automobiles or railroad cars to save the life of a loved one, even if the effort causes them to shred themselves internally. To avoid tapping into this deep reserve and turning your intestines into linguine, stack your bones and you'll be able to make it upright to the closing bell.

Old Ladies, Little Cloud
Courtesy of Powder Shots

"Guru" Dave extracting a few samples for later analysis
Courtesy of D2X

Chips to Who Dunnit

Chips is the placid groomer on the skier's right side of Peruvian Gulch

Chapter 14

On Drifting

While the concept of carving has been around for as long as skiers have been sliding across snow, it has achieved the status of a religion since shaped (aka "carving") skis achieved market dominance in the new millennium. Carving is goodness, truth and beauty. The alternative is skidding, a pejorative term connoting a loss of control, a trajectory determined more by chance than by the force of will and sinew. But carving is not an Absolute Good. It is a rule meant to be broken, a vow given with a wink.

One reason carving gets all the good press is that it needs to be taught, while any other form of sliding around comes more or less naturally. Little wonder carving has a superiority complex. But the dirty little secret inside carving cant is that most carved turns begin with a bit of drift, an off-the-edge moment when anything is possible. This isn't a flaw as much as a natural interval that lives in the transition between turns. The drift can be as ephemeral as a hummingbird's heartbeat or a long, lingering note hung out to dry in the mountain air. Drifting is skidding with intention, a choice to slither instead of slice.

By breaking up carving's monopoly on well-respected turns, drifting opens the door to an alternative sensation, the sideward slide. When applied to a swath of corn snow, it builds up its own wave, shedding snow off the base in soft curls the consistency of ice cream. By the next day, yesterday's corn will have frozen to a titanium rigidity you couldn't indent with a pile driver. Again, the drift comes to the rescue: instead of trying to cut into the crystalline crust, you tilt your bases until the ski is almost on edge, but not quite. Applying pressure to the base where the edge isn't – the un-edge, if you'll pardon the expression – you grind across the slick, implacable surface, draining the velocity that would otherwise accelerate you to light speed on a clean, carved edge.

Executed with the appropriate aplomb, the drift is also a tactic to conserve precious energy. Drifting raises just standing around to an art form: you try, as elegantly as possible, to do next to nothing. This talent is essential if you're going to consume this giant mountain in one gulp. The non-stop express run is woven into the fabric of this place, if for no other reason than the only way to catch the same tram again is to race it to the bottom. But there is another reason: the non-stop is the ultimate expression of visualizing the bottom of the hill. This ability to intuit, not merely the next turn, but all succeeding turns, is the essence of following the flow, of blending doing and being into one indivisible form of energy. This will perforce require the application of every turn in your arsenal, including the tactical drift. Carving requires the pilot to resist forces that strive to scrub him or her laterally; drifting surrenders to them. As long as you remain the calm center in the heart of the drift, the energy cycle running through you will align with your stacked bones. All your muscles have to do is keep you casually upright.

Yet the drift is more than a tactic to conserve energy; it's a natural expression of being in the flow, a syncopation of the beat that allows you to match the cadence of the hill. Drift and drive. Slink, then tilt and push where the mountain asks you to. It's a breath of relaxation, an opportunity to contemplate exactly when to shift from drift to drive. The slide supplies a momentary suspension in the downhill attack, the cleansing inhalation, a pause at the top of the cycle of effort.

Even when you're schwagging – contemporary parlance for the uncarved turn - you don't have to abandon the idea of roundness. Au contraire, you may find more roundness in a sweet, buttery drift than an abruptly edged, laid-over arc. Drifting is the optimal way to steer into your desired alignment with the hill, as in when diving into a run like Mark Malu or Regulator Johnson that enters off a traverse, then igniting the arrow. You drift then stick to grab the force of linearity again, the locked-on laser that bends with the terrain.

The advent of the fully rockered, twin-tipped fat ski ensures that drifting, smearing, buttering, schwagging, grinding and schmearing will be with us for the foreseeable future. These skis *can* be carved, believe it or not, even on crispy corduroy, but that is not their bliss. They are meant to be swiveled, shmooshed and skittered. The twin-tip alone is an open invitation to linger in the smear zone between forward and backward. Jacking the tips and tails out of the snow with formidable front and rear rocker makes the platform underfoot barely longer than your boot, the better to smudge in any direction. Now plump up the ski waist over 120mm and you have a stick that threatens to blow out both knees if you attempt to tilt it all the way up on edge. Little wonder when you see America's youth rocketing backwards downhill they never seem to be on edge; they're not.

They're butter boys and girls, so accustomed to the schmear and the grind they only resort to an edged turn when they can't afford to shed speed. Ah, sweet mystery of youth!

If the terrain park is where the drift dawdles, in the moguls it lasts no longer than a spark. But it's there, not as a lateral smudge, but a weightless microsecond when both skis are flat and can be pivoted effortlessly to fine-tune the top of the next turn. The more liquid skiers can ineffably insinuate their skis into any line because they can blend the swivel of the schmear and the stick of the carve at will. The moment can be so quick, it's invisible even to the skier, yet in its perfect, invisible execution lies greatness.

Perhaps nowhere is the drift at the top of nearly every turn so evident as it is in deep powder. Anyone who has mastered this condition knows there can be a pause, a taffy-pulled beat when you must be patient before the plunge and let flat skis float back under you before you bet the moon on your next move. Wait for it, wait for it – and while you wait, your skis are slipping through the transition, as flat as Kansas – then the command to tilt takes charge as both skis roll to edges that might as well be pushing against silence.

If drifting in powder elicits the susurrating sounds of silk slapping skin, drifting on early-AM boilerplate is as loud as the front row at a Metallica concert. In late spring, the dreamy corn of yesterday is the ice-slick brick of the next morning. If one ventures down Chips - the normally benign cruiser that is the least adventurous descent on the front face - before the sun has had a chance to soften it, you are well advised to shelve all notions of carving it up. Now is the time to discover the phantom crown on your base, a point somewhere between the middle and the nearest edge to the snow, which you can set at a fixed angle and stand on. Try not to let your movements betray the fact that you have only a tenuous grip on trajectory. Shift your weight and direction when the mountain tells you to and suppress the notion that a better person would have carved their way down. In due course the surface consistency will change from metallic to more mushy and edges can again be engaged in the business of tucking into each arc.

As you wend your way towards the lower mountain, keep your eyes out skier's right for the nearly 90° turnoff to Who Dunnit. This oft-overlooked, low-angle cruiser is comfort for tired legs and solace for the troubled soul. It lies at a slight angle to the fall line so every right turn curls uphill and every left falls away. If you can't hear the rhythm of this run talk to you, you should get your hearing checked. Where the top of Chips was a glass lake, this is a stream of love butter, each turn a caress stroked in cadence with the hill.

Far from being a sin, drifting is part of the sensory delight of skiing. It's a reminder, as we feel the soft snow slide across our bases, that we are here to make bliss. Heaven knows we're not making anything else. At the end of the day, we've made no product, conquered no disease, saved no one from hunger. All we did was make bliss, and it was enough. We found a way to experience joy in harmony both with nature and ourselves. For a few minutes we disappeared, part of an energy field in which we were more conduit than controller. Somewhere in that thread lay a perfect moment when identity folded into doing, when all there was in the world was the call of the mountain and your reply, an echo that sounded like joy. The suggestion the mountain planted in you, in us all, is to tuck these moments into your soul where they will reverberate forever with its message: those with the capacity for such joy have the obligation to share it.

Bananas Trees off Gad 2

Vanessa Aadland running through the woods

Photo by Jay Dash

Chapter 15

On Trees

The trees were here first, and so perhaps it's fitting they should provide the last shelter, the forested fortress to which we resort when all other venues have been trampled into submission. In the trees we can still find, tucked around the next corner, a pillow of essence preserved just for us. The trees are the guardians of the last stash.

They are also the cure for vertigo. When storms settle into this canyon, the most open expanses on the upper mountain are exercises in minimalist art, alabaster on ecru, with every normally discernable detail eradicated. This has a disabling effect on the inner ear, which sends an urgent message to the optic nerve to give it a reference, anything that will shed light on which way is down. The trees know, and are happy to oblige. Their magnificent immobility provides an axis around which our vastly diminished universe can orbit.

When we're in the trees, they become the center of our turns, the radial point around which we rotate. They live in the center because we cannot permit them to intersect the perimeter. When we are in motion in the woods, the trees become dark matter, substance seen yet not encountered, light's dark twin. For the way to ski the trees is to seek the edge of light, the blush of photons on an evergreen limb that promises an opening, an invitation to stay in the flow where rhythm and faith guide our descent.

Visualization and anticipation have their limitations in the trees, as it's *ipso facto* difficult to see very far ahead. Proceeding apace is a matter of belief, a safe, forward projection of the self in time and space. We continue because we know the coast is clear; whatever obstacle appears around the next corner, we will have all the time we need to avoid. Trees somehow induce the concentration it requires to ski them; we focus so intently on a path we cannot see that the veil of self-consciousness is stripped away. We become our movements, beings of pure sensation.

The trick to skiing the trees is to not be in a hurry. There's enough room, there's enough time, as long as you move in the path the trees have allowed, which is usually not the fast lane. When you find the rhythm of the forest, your line keeps opening up before you, as if the trees were guiding you. If you also sense that they are protecting you, it's because they are. The woods are a sanctuary from wind and an oasis of visibility when the rest of the world is plunged in whiteness.

The trees want us to succeed. They understand our role in the energy flow, how we nourish the mountain who is their matriarch. Why else would they exchange the vile gas we exhale for sweet, fresh oxygen, if not to sustain us? We are not the only beings with a purpose to their presence here.

The trees shape the notes; our paths through them share the silences where they resonate. We move in the hallways the trees left for themselves, their public space, territory they own even if they don't presently occupy it. As we trespass their property, we ski the trees by ignoring them, by setting our energy radar for the next glimmer of light and willing ourselves through it. To stare at a tree while in flight is to grant it the power of attraction, the amazing facility an animated but immobilized entity has to pull us into its thrall. Treat each tree as if it were Medusa and look anywhere but at it.

Skiing the trees is about being fluid and elastic, about feeling, about heart telling head to go take a shower. If your monkey mind is chattering away, you won't feel small changes in the slope underneath, your best information source in a world that may not extend more than a few feet ahead. When your mind gets quiet you can see the softer shade of green, reflected light off evergreen boughs, indicating the slit-wide opening to the path ahead. Each flicker of light is a promise, each arc an expectation, catalyzed by the endorphin rush of sinking into satin snow.

On an overcast, blustery day when the light is flat, it's time to head for the Bananas Trees off the top of the Gad 2 chair. The snow the wind has removed from the exposed slopes will have loaded into the woods, so it should be safe to pick any entry point skier's left off Gadzooks, but exercise some caution as the line is steep, rolling and slightly off camber. The tree spacing is gracious but irregular and gets tight here and there. Keep your shoulders square to the hill and your feet ready to dance. The slope angle will naturally feed you towards Bananas, but if you veer off skier's right and cross Gadzooks, you'll discover the oft-overlooked Bananas Bowl. A line of trees blocks a clear view of the entry, so look for a substantial piece of artillery as your gateway indicator. The top of the bowl drops off steeply, but it's a clean, open shot with plenty of room to run until you re-connect either with Gadzooks or the northwest-facing tree lines skier's right of Lift Line. As the relentless steeps finally start to flatten out, bleed some speed or you may hit a cat-track by surprise, providing an unforgettable moment. To scope out the various tree lines between Lift Line and S.T.H., give the area a close inspection from the Gad 2 chair, which we recommend you board again, for the trees always reserve a powder pocket for those with the will to find it.

Many generations ago, men believed trees held the memory of all the events to which they have been witness. Whether you still believe that or not, surely the tree stores some record within each band that marks its annual growth. Trees are children of the circle, upright echoes of the giant vortex generators they anchor. When we move through their space with focused minds and open hearts, the awe we feel is like being in a cathedral or other holy monument, sensing the presence of spirits that we feel as a heightened acuity, a sharper attention to detail, and suddenly yet unhurriedly the line ahead is clear. We slide among the sentinels to our history, writing our own transient footnote below their vaulted, vibrating canopy.

The forest provides a refuge from more than just weather. It's an arena for sounds we can't hear, for a silence that seems alive. We live in a very noisy world, bombarding some of our senses into dysfunction. The trees absorb all the sound in our spectrum and in their encompassing silence create a retreat where we can rediscover reverence. In return, the trees grant us some of their grounding, trying to teach us to understand where we stand.

Let the light be your guide through the trees

Wilbere Lift

Total immersion

Photographer: Eric Hostetler

Chapter 16

On Sensuality

Skiing is not like other forms of exercise. It's a physically demanding activity, as beginners in particular can attest, but it isn't anything like working out. It's a public display that's intrinsically private, a mental game requiring physical expertise, a form of self-expression not just performed *on* the medium of snow but *in* it. Like all moments when we surrender to bliss, skiing involves a disappearing act, a submersion in the moment, a letting go of identity that accompanies the most intense feelings of being alive.

The essence of sensuality is touching, contact between our bodies and the world that reassures us we are really here. In the White World, touch isn't limited to our fingertips; we feel the snow from the soles of our feet to the patches on our cheeks that bear the brunt of face shots. We feel snow in a way football players don't feel the field, or figure skaters experience ice or skydivers interact with the air. Snow isn't like anything else. It begins as an idea within the most undifferentiated of media – water - every molecule monotonously identical, and turns it into an unrivaled celebration of individuality. What could be more like us, essentially all the same yet no two samples alike? Little wonder the snow knows how to please us.

Our rapport with the snow parallels the *pas de deux* of human relationships. We want it to embrace us but not confine us, let us run but hold us back, and most of all to caress us, to gently but firmly define the limits of our beings. When weightless Wasatch white washes up the inner thigh, the intention of intimacy is unmistakable. What more does a mountain have to do to get our attention?

Sensuality is both a reward and a state of being in which every sensory gateway is flung wide open. The inbound flood of sensations triggers the joy factories in the brain to double their output. When dropping from turn to turn on a steep powder run, the cycle of rise, float, fall and finish is accompanied by the sound of skis blasting through the essence, ripping the snow into the air and forming it into a funnel that trails behind us like glory. In that moment we become the center of a universe of one, more a presence than a person, a vessel through which energy flows with the speed of light. Our internal clocks slow down. Our bodies move freely, unimpeded by supervision, our busy minds having grown quiet. When we hit the apron and gravity's stream turns to a trickle, the tide of elation takes minutes to subside.

The unpleasant sensation that the air seems suddenly out of oxygen serves as a reminder that for the last couple of minutes we've been so marinated in the moment we forgot to breathe. Exhaustion and ecstasy compete for our attention. This is the customary coda to sex, to which skiing is often favorably compared. Certainly skiing is less messy, both literally and metaphorically. Skiing also offers greater variety without complications and higher frequency without pills. And skiing will never break your heart.

Sensuality is a two-way street, both touching and being touched. The snow, the air, the chill; all touch us everywhere with everything they've got. When we touch back, it's mostly with our feet, not usually our preferred appendage for applying a light stroke. That distinction belongs to our hands, our most versatile sensuality delivery system. What are these normally active players up to while we ski?

Our hands conduct the music of our descent, finding a melody in the ether the rest of the body can dance to. They also help to point us forward and hold us in overall balance, just as they do for the tightrope walker. To provide both balance and beat, hands have to be held in an arc between our hips and our hearts. When they operate near our center of power they keep us unshakably on course. The streams we ride on big mountains aren't placid canals; they're raging torrents driven by the energy of the vortex and convoluted by writhing variations in the terrain. It takes calm, temperate hands to conduct your concerto in this tempest.

The momentary amnesia induced by our surrender to sensuality is the payoff for our relationship with the mountain. For a period of time we can never accurately measure, we stop mediating experience and become what we are doing. We are sensation without judgment, joy without restraint, energy without boundaries. The snow is our lover of a thousand hands, lifting us up, bathing us gently, wrapping us in its cool coils of coruscating confetti. We are compelled to see her again and again, like an addiction.

Sensuality bestows presence, the rare combination of focus on the now, or where we stand in time, wedded to a keen awareness of where we stand in space. To savor the succulence of presence, let's envision a run on a powder morning that won't attract the crazed crowd in the overflowing Tram line. Slink the other way, over the bridge and up to the access road that leads to the Wilbere lift, where only a handful of folks wait for it to open. The ride up is painfully slow, providing ample opportunity to peruse the lines through the trees looker's right of the lift line, with the aspens on the west-facing aspects appearing particularly promising. As you get off the lift, you'll see the groomed promenade of Wilbere Ridge to your right and to your left, wide-open fields of dreams filled with two hours' worth of uncut snow crystals.

The only feature that will interrupt your downhill indulgence is the Bass Highway cat-track that cuts the fall line in two. To integrate this hiccup into the sensuous flow of your run, anticipate your arrival at the road so you come off the pitch in the middle of a turn. Let your skis drift a bit to absorb this kink in your kinetics, then shift your weight forward so you drop off the road just as you drop into your next arc. Being smooth through a rough transition is all about timing and feeling, the underlying mechanics of sensuality.

Sensuality is sensation raised to the level of rapture. It's there for us to experience every time we step into gravity's stream, re-establishing our relationship with the mountain. The attainment of sensuality that allows our conscious selves to evaporate under the spell of the moment depends on the pure intentions of both partners. Ideally, we give in to the flow of the mountain and the mountain, accepting our surrender, allows us to caress her with our turns.

The Goo encoiled in rings of fluffulescence.
Courtesy of Powder Shots

Restaurant Chutes off Mid-Cirque Traverse

Gate to High Baldy

Jaws, Upper Cirque

Checking out the entry to the Upper Cirque

Chapter 17

Don't Feed the Fear Puppy

Fear is like a lost puppy in a horror movie: you innocently start to feed it, soon it won't leave you alone then it grows up to eat you alive. It's very important you don't feed the puppy.

The big problem with fear, aside from the feelings of uncontrollable terror, is that we don't work very well when we're petrified. If you remained awake during junior high geology, you'll recall that petrified objects do not move well. Normally, the only way out of a predicament gnarly enough to raise a knot of fear is some sort of physical activity, which is going to be awfully challenging if you're as flexible as bronze. The only way you're getting down is if you find some deep chamber inside where you can lure your fear, lock it up and ignore its raging long enough to get the task at hand accomplished.

When fear muscles its way to the front of the conscious mind, it tends to imbue the obstacles we face with special powers held in reserve just to defeat us. But what are we really afraid of? It's not the obstacles in front of us, be they cliff or cornice or kicker. Fear doesn't reside in things; it lives in us. That's why it can be so overpowering: what terrifies lies within. And the more we feed it, the more it grows.

It's very hard to trick our bodies into believing we're ready when our brains are standing on the brakes. If the mind isn't focused on a positive outcome, this movie isn't going to have a Disney ending. Start the healing process by focusing on the details. Let's pull a few samples from the Fear Factory production line and see how dialing down to details can defang them.

Let's begin with a bone-jarring if otherwise uneventful ride along the spine of the Cirque Traverse. This is a well-worn line, both by traffic and pulverizing winds, so follow along the ridge a little to the left and lower than the most exposed route. Suppose the face on the Mid Cirque is trenched to ribbons, so you search further downhill for a line through the trees on your left. And there it is, a sucker line into the Restaurant Chutes that shows no sign of previous passage, pulling you into trees that at first beckon with open lines but soon shut down until the next turn is a mystery.

You hit the brakes as if a baby stroller just rolled in front of your SUV. You're in forest thick enough to disorient Sacajawea and to make life more interesting, you stand on a small rock band. You could try climbing up and out, but out where? (If Gertrude Stein were in the same predicament, she'd say there was no out out.) You look down. The ground isn't far away, but neither are the evergreens. The fear generating inside you is fueled by the realization that you are going to have to jump. And land. And not rocket straight into the next pine tree.

For one particularly grim moment, you wonder how the patrol is ever going to cart your carcass out of here, assuming they find you. So buck up, cowboy, failure is not an option. You can't just slide off the cliff band like a sack of potatoes. So what does success look like? You back up a step to allow yourself to go off straight, in line with the only landing zone. You see yourself picking up your feet, hands forward, extending for the ground, hitting, aiming for the white area between the bark columns and braking with a sudden sink of the feet. Focusing on the details reduces the amount of room within which fear has to operate.

The Gad Chutes in low snow conditions

If you can see it in every detail, you can do it. Turn the fact that you have to get this right into an advantage. This is a life moment. How are you going to deal with it? The ten-foot fall in front of you won't take a second. Really, all you have to do is not freak out. Just be active. Don't be a victim. PICK UP YOUR DAMN FEET. One at a time, if that makes the moment feel more natural, just don't go over the brink passively, like luggage. Spot the landing, hit the landing; now you're a skier again, so ski. You'll miss the tree as long as you don't try too hard to hit it. If you concentrate on the outcome, fear can't find its way in.

You're down in one piece, although now all your pieces fit together better. You're not the same person who stood over a rock band mere seconds ago, frozen with the realization that you were all in, holding a hand with no aces. You visualized, you committed, you stuck it. It's how Superboy must have felt when he realized he could fly. If you can manage not to feed the fear puppy, there's no telling how far you can fly.

Fear can sneak up on you, catching you in that instant when you move one way and fate moves another. Suppose it's a storm day and word circulates on the tram that the short trek to High Baldy is about to open. You bolt in that direction only to find the gate closed. So maybe you're a bit distracted as you follow the rope line down to a flat zone where the wind has left its calling card, a 4-foot drift that blocks your path to Plan B. When you pick up speed to punch through it, you don't anticipate one ski being yanked off course into a tree well while the other augers into the thick windcrust, sending you headfirst into the hollow moat that rings a giant pine.

Falls, by definition, are uncontrolled events. If you could have controlled the whiplash gymnastics that deposited you upside down, your knees contorted painfully above your head, with apparently no bottom to the infinite powder accumulation engulfing you, you would have. The deep snow covers you in a suffocating quilt of its ultra-cold essence. Your knees are screaming in the concrete, sub-zero grip of the wind wave and there isn't a chance in hell of releasing your bindings, because you haven't an ounce of leverage.

No bottom, no bottom, no bottom, drowning... The wind shovels the snow back in your face as fast as you can push it away, flailing for a breath, precious breath. A wild panic reigns; surges of adrenaline flush your blood stream, sending hot waves of flashing frenzy to fuel the flailing. "This is no good," you think, as you're alone, with no one to hear you even if you could call for help. Your thrashing works you deeper and deeper into the white quicksand.

You confront the grisly paradox of your predicament: more manic movement will induce more mini snow slides. How to quell energy-sapping fear at this critical juncture? Be calm, be calm, think now, think, think, calm down, breathe, breathe, get quiet, find your center, ignore the pain and the thought that your knee is going to blow itself to bits as you hang by its ligaments, but you have to get quiet. An idea filters into consciousness. You work with the only purchase available, the tree branches. Reach out and up, extend, grab a branch and pull. Do it again. Movement, yes, but no progress. Again panic takes over and you feel a hot flash that makes you colder than the weather, with the ripe sweat of effort evaporating. When your next burst of energy sails into the universe unharnessed, you come to the realization that panic lacks credentials as a problem-solver.

You'll have to reach deeper to find the positive aspects of a fearfully negative now. First plus, you can breathe. Second bonus, you're still in a location where someone might happen by, although with the gate above you closed that's unlikely. And third favorable factor, you're still intact, essentially uninjured. So you recover your composure. It's time to WORK THE PROBLEM. That's all you have, all there is in what's left of your world, so work the problem. Grab that branch again and make it work. Bit by bit, snow begins to pack under you, scant progress, some improvement, but at this rate...

That's not the point; each little bit adds up. Finally, sweat pouring over cold skin, you gain traction and begin to ease the strain on aggravated sinews, working your way to the point where you can draw on the last reserves of stamina, regaining an upright stance, whence you can release your bindings and extract your ski tips from the grip of the wind-slab monster. Spent, you ease your way upright towards Plan B, a shot that still has your name on it, and here you embrace the experience of the descent, propelled by the discharge stored from the last 45 minutes mining the energy field. You are free, merely strained and drained, but you've surmounted fear, or False Evidence Appearing Real. You've had to dig deep, but that's what many life-in-the-balance situations demand. This place, so rarely encountered, presents the extraordinary occasion to find the strength, perseverance and vision mandated by the moment to surmount dire circumstances that morph from a potentially catastrophic situation to a sort of resurrection, a deeper awareness of what it means to be present.

This new awareness is akin to opening a new bank account in which a fortune has been deposited in your name. You can draw on it anytime. Just the awareness that salvation lies not in the first reach, but in incremental grasps, in the accumulation of effort, informs every heartbeat thereafter. The branch you grasp, the link that brings you back, is the life force itself. There will be other occasions when unforeseen events spin out of control, times when it will be useful to know that at the heart of every tree well is a tree that points the way out.

Fear is episodic, anecdotal, personal. A friend steps on an unseen rock at the very brink of Jaws on the Upper Cirque. Thrown headlong off the precipice, he ragdolls out of sight. Several feet below, his torn-off ski protrudes from a wall of rime-covered rocks. You are the last man uphill. It's on you.

You drop into the next line over where the cover is better and cut back, over the spine separating the chutes and park below the rock face where the lost ski has taken temporary residence. The only way up is with skis off, so you set your skis up where they might break your fall if you lose your footing, then begin to pick your way up. The face is ridiculously steep. You are in race boots, the mountaineering equivalent of glass slippers. Every new step crunches the fragile snow layer that formed the last buffer between plastic and see-through ice. There is no retracing a single step, not now, not on the return trip. With each step, the ski seems to move farther uphill. You are out of excellent options.

Each step is an existential voyage: who are you, and will whoever you are be able to make it the next step? Finally, you have the ski, and carefully pull it free, fighting to keep from tilting one degree further backward and into free fall. You'd love to carry the ski back down to your shaken and stirred friend, but your feet are blind and lubricious so you'll need all the hands you have. The ski is sent tail-first downward, where it sinks like an arrow into the pitch below. You move after it like a gecko, all fingertips and toes, feeling for a fresh surface, and deliverance.

Photographer: Eric Hostetler
Bracing for a wind berm in Baldy

Wherever the Music of the Mountain is Loudest

The sky harmonizing with the music of Twin Peaks,
viewed from the Gadzoom lift.

Chapter 18

On Music

In the un-White World there is rarely a moment when we can filter out all the static energy that surrounds us and experience silence. So we play music and play it loud, the better to drown out the noise; but all we've done is add another layer – albeit a pleasurable one - to the din. Is it any wonder then, that when we head to the mountains we bring our habits and our music with us, our defense against an invasive world? We cocoon ourselves in an envelope of soothing sound, incubated by imported rhythms. No matter how exquisite or sublime, the music we wear like a shield isn't the music of the mountain. Be here now. Hear the music of where you are.

The White World emits sounds all its own, beats of energy that can only be heard in the quiet. The White World tries to teach us to be still so we can hear its soft music. In the rare air of altitude these powerful vibrations travel great distances, so they are accessible for all to hear, but they can't complete the transmission if a collision of sounds already occupy the ears of the internalized. Put away the iPod, Luke, and let the force be with you.

If you put down your imported music, if you can leave it behind in the un-White World that spawned it, you'll find the first natural notes you hear are products of the wind. The wind operates its music factory on two levels, the general and the specific, or more accurately, the public and the personal. On a grand scale, the wind uses every feature on the mountain to create its own calliope, blasting out notes that can be heard as far away as Cottonwood. These top notes are accompanied by the private music it reserves for each individual as he slices through the activated air. The personal notes are more interesting because they're more variable, subject to change with a turn of the head. As one ear cavitates in relation to the wind, creating an aural eddy of lower vibrations, the opposite ear hears a higher frequency; together, the wind song forms a symphony by one, of one and for one. These are *your* sounds, music composed and performed by your movements. Like the sounds of breaking waves or a gurgling stream, these natural rhythms can have a mesmerizing effect, slipping us into a state where our mind is less busy, more focused and calm. In the quiet, you can hear sound not just in your ears but beneath your skin, a sonic pulse that plays a duet with your signature life force.

The sounds your skis create as they impact the snow hold a data mine of information. Skis are tuning forks we get to ride, notes just waiting to be played. A switch in their sonic pitch presages a shift in the snow surface; a staccato vibrato sings a song of boilerplate frozen to the hardness of tungsten. The soft, long notes of corn snow instill the certainty that almost any turn will hold its course. The purr that powder makes as your skis plow it aside is cut from the same sensory cloth as the low, reverent notes murmured by a chorus of monks. With each turn, your voice harmonizes with theirs. Only when you stop do you realize how loudly the music of angels rang in your ears, singing a melody meant for your ears only.

The music of your skis, emanating from each caress of the mountain, overlays shattered-crystal treble notes on the wind song. The crush of steel on crystals of essence releases vibrations of Wagnerian power, connecting to that primal part of us that detects disturbances in the ether. This interactive song, created by your interplay with all the forces loose on the mountain, taps into a wellspring of joy so intense you may have to give it voice, the final, ecstatic note of your own, elemental symphony.

The sonata the mountain sings to us isn't military music with its strident, changeless beat. The mountain stores an eclectic selection of playlists, but none of its emanations are as monotonous as a metronome. Point being, the mountain shouldn't be skied that way. Disobey the drill sergeant in your head. *Stop making turns.* Don't play scales, play the concerto of gravity's stream, let the energy flow from your skis, up your stacked bones and through the top of your head.

We are made of energy. We ski because when we do we rediscover this essential truth. When we ski well we become pure vessels of force, photons in a beam of light shining from the base of the tetrahedron, both wave and particle, both music and the beam it rides upon, shining endlessly through space-time. Herein lies the secret of the mountain: *we are but notes*, musical fragments in a song of unimaginable beauty this mountain sends out to this precious universe. We may be the inaudible tree falling in an empty forest, but still we, like the mountain upon which we stand, strive to be heard.

This is why we feel the vibration of the mountain beneath the skin, because it's coursing through every corpuscle, activating every axon that makes up what we call a self. The cadence of the mountain isn't a metaphor, a game of the imagination played to trick us into believing we can connect to a stupendous pile of rock and crystals. It's as real as mathematics or cymatics, the proof that music *is* geometry, that all that separates sound from solid is our inability to see the connection.

Once we know that all that we imagine to be substantial is made up of notes, all that is left to discover is the plasticity of time. This awareness also lies before us with the clarity of light itself: when we move at speeds humanoids were never meant to, we discover in the still center that time is elastic. We have all the time that we need. Good thing, because that's all we're going to get.

How is it possible, that standing on a harmonic device made to ride a curved surface over an inverted funnel, we can feel such completion? Is it a bribe from the mountain, a payoff, a yummy treat to encourage us to ride the cycle again to the top? Do you notice how the same soul that arrived two seconds ago on the Plaza, spent, his mortal coil melting into his boots, suddenly finds the wherewithal to scramble after the next tram? Tent revivalists wouldn't have the audacity to conjure such a metamorphosis, yet it happens with the regularity of an all-prune diet.

When you let the mountain decide the cadence of your arc and its energy flows through you unimpeded, every beat builds the puissance of its antipodes. The mountain pulls your energy on the downbeat and sends it back with vigorish at the top. The ski hums its programmed harmony, letting the light and vibration pass through as if it were an extension, not just of your body, but of your spirit. As you stand on the absolute center, energy flows so smoothly in all directions that you feel the magnificent equanimity of light, traveling infinitely in all directions without losing focus. That part of you that is still sensationally flesh feels nothing but the sensuality of soft snow sloughing off the edge. It's such an overflowing feeling you may start laughing with joy you can no longer contain.

People wouldn't keep returning to this mystic center if they weren't getting the message. The music of this place is theirs as well, as it was before they were born, as it will be centuries from now. The sounds of the mountain are our vibrations, our notes, being played by everyone's participation in the dance, right now, for our ears only, for we are the notes we hear.

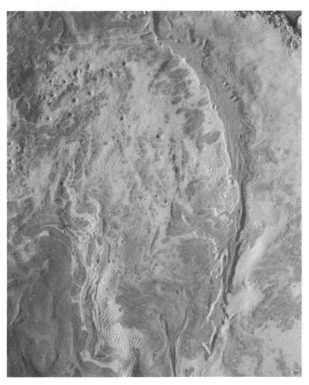

Painting of a phrase of celestial music by D. Powers

Silver Fox Cliffs

Silver Fox Cliffs

Chapter 19

On Gratitude
&
Asking Permission

"It's more, I'd say, not so much a word as kind of a state of consciousness that I try to get into and it has to do with a – I'm not trying to sound too weird – it's tuning into the earth and her spirit. I ask the earth a lot if it's safe to go over here or go over there, things like that. The things that guide me are these vibrations that I feel, these frequencies of light that go through my body. I've had plenty of experiences that justify this. I've been in really weird situations and been told not to go there [by the earth], and sure enough, I shouldn't have."
– **Scot Schmidt in Greg Stump's** ***The Legend of Aahhhs***

When someone has learned to listen to light, it's wise to listen to him. Pay close attention to these words from the man who redefined the boundaries of freeskiing, a transcendent talent who introduced the term "extreme" into the sporting lexicon. He taught himself how to clear his mind so he could pick up vibrations from the mountain, vibrations he experienced as light coursing through him, which would tell him if and where it was safe to proceed. It speaks volumes about his character that he arrived at this understanding solely through communion with the earth. It's also highly instructive that after thousands of runs - 90% of which all skiers couldn't even contemplate without injury - Scot Schmidt has never been hurt.

This absence of debilitating accidents is not a coincidence. Scot Schmidt has remained injury-free because he is always humble before the mountain, because he asks its permission to go. When he drops in some perilous chute, he succeeds not just because he has visualized what he must do, but because in a sense he has already done it: the idea is already whole and complete, awaiting only his actions to manifest it. He moves as instructed by the light. How amazing and perfect is that?

The chances of anyone learning to ski like Scot Schmidt are virtually nil – no one has managed the feat in the 25 years since his skiing was first put on exhibit before a slack-jawed public. But everyone can learn to think like him. Everyone can learn humility before the mountain.

Nowhere is this more important than at Snowbird, where if you don't approach the mountain with the appropriate measure of humility, the mountain will be more than happy to supply some. Take your eye off the ball here by celebrating your brilliance prematurely and humility will be the next course served.

A corollary to humility is respect, the implicit acknowledgement that we share the planet with others and owe our brethren a dollop of deference. Respect is commonly demonstrated by displaying good manners, and the first article of appropriate behavior is expressing gratitude. Yet how many times a day do we benefit from the grace of this mountain without remembering to say, "Thank you?" Regrettably, it's far more likely to overhear boasts in the tram line such as, "Did you see the way I stomped that line?" To which we say, first of all, big deal. Secondly, where is the respect, the humility or the gratitude in this attitude? All these attributes require the ability to consider the needs and desires of others as of at least equal value as one's own, a sentiment expressed in pubic places as courtesy. Yet our national "me-first" obsession has made manners as obsolete as alchemy.

Let us share another secret from a couple of lifetimes devoted to skiing: all the very greatest skiers are like Schmidt. They are humble, respectful and courteous. Again, not an accident. The proud, the loud and the rude will never achieve communion with the mountain and will never understand why they are here. But here they are, and so we, along with the mountain, must teach them the rules of behavior. This isn't an option. We all have to actively remind people of how to behave because, simply put, lives are at stake.

The two most likely ways to meet one's end on the mountain are via avalanche or collision. While there are obscure exceptions, such sad events are usually the result of a failure to show proper respect, either to the mountain or to fellow citizens. We can't hurtle downhill side by side at 40 mph if we don't bring an attitude of sharing to the slopes. If all we are listening to is the noise in our heads, not only will we never achieve communion with the mountain, we'll be a menace to mankind.

If you took the counsel of curmudgeons, you'd blame kids today. But gratitude and courtesy aren't generational attributes: the elderly can be obnoxious and the young can be contemplative and kind. Take the case of Oakley White-Allen, a 33-year old who began exploring this mountain five years ago. One recent winter there dawned a day when the snow was especially heinous. On the front face, a few paltry inches of low-density dust barely disguised a 40° skating rink, cleverly constructed by the rains that had deluged the peak two days prior. One false move and you'd punch through the irregular crust, turning your shin into the impromptu prow of an icebreaker. Humility was the norm on Upper Silver Fox, where arrhythmic bumps were barely disguised by this 3-layer dip from hell. The run had become an unskiable morass of hideosity from top to bottom.

Then along comes Oakley. He doesn't tiptoe in to get a sense of the snowpack, he launches. He motors through the upper moguls as if they were a mirage, then just before he reaches the trees that punctuate the lower cliff bands, he throws it in reverse without shedding a shred of speed. Now scorching the hill switch, Oakley aims for the tallest pile of rock and – bing! – tosses an insouciant off-axis air, landing backwards and sailing into Chips Flats as if he hadn't a care in the world.

Asked later how he managed to slay that line in conditions no one else could even hack their way through, Oakley replied, "I asked for the mountain's permission."

You won't ski like Oakley just by asking the mountain's permission, but you'll never ski anything like your best if you don't. Remember, the mountain knows you're here; it feels you in its stream. The mountain appreciates manners even if you don't. Remember to say "please" and "thank you" and the mountain will return gifts of miraculous value.

Lenny Johnson, 81, who has skied Snowbird for the last 22 years and is thankful for every one of them, experienced just such a miraculous gift. It happened on the same run, Silver Fox, where we just described Oakley's exploits. Picking his way down through a wind-swept snowstorm, Lenny momentarily came to rest by a hollow the wind had carved out of the slope. For some reason, he paused and looked in the hollow and there, shivering with cold, was a tiny, pink-nosed mouse. The mouse made no move to run, but kept its quivering gaze fixed on Lenny. In their shared moment the world was reduced to the two of them, and a connection was forged. Lenny knew that he could have been that mouse, and suddenly he felt what it was like to be isolated, terrified and so very dependent.

So he reached down to the mouse, who made no effort to move away. Lenny slid his cupped palm under the miniscule creature and scooped it up. It remained calm in his custody as he traversed skier's right across the hill to a small copse of evergreens where he found a nook where he could deposit the mouse. There was never any question of doing otherwise, for to deny the mouse its chance for survival he'd have to exchange his own capacity for compassion. For some reason, the mountain connected Lenny and that mouse on a frequency – like Schmidt's frequency – that normally resides outside the range of human detection. Maybe Lenny needed a metaphysical reminder meant just for him, but for whatever reason that moment of connection remains a resonant chord in Lenny's soul that will vibrate forever.

What is the source of such serendipity and synchronicity? Lenny appeared because the mouse needed him. The mouse appeared to Lenny for the reciprocal reason. We know how Lenny found his way to the mouse. But how did the mouse ever find this intersection with Lenny? How does any bite-sized mouse navigate across Silver Fox in the dead of winter during a blazing snowstorm? It should have been swept to Provo. Yet it was there for Lenny to find and save, so Lenny could be found and saved.

Lenny is fond of saying, "I can never give back all this mountain has given me. I can never thank it enough." And so he has thanked it every day, honoring those gifts it has bestowed on him. Should we really be so surprised the mountain sent a Lenny a mouse to say, "You're welcome?

Mach Schnell

Mach Schnell's wall-to-wall bumps are rimmed by trees.

Chapter 20

On the Advantages of Being a Two-Footed Animal

Darwinists quite correctly coo over the evolutionary edge provided by opposable thumbs, but as skiers we're just as grateful for feet, opposable big toes or no. We also give thanks that said two feet are separately wired, each able to respond to a different set of instructions. When the contrasting commands are issued in panic mode, the results can be calamitous, but when sublimely coordinated the result is the serenity of an endless edge.

There has probably been more ski instruction flapdoodle generated about when and how to shift weight from one foot to another than on any other subject in the instructional canon because this movement is the essence of the turn and the turn is the Grail of instruction. The truth possesses an economy of ideas in inverse proportion to the volume of cant; it is a whisper of simplicity. *Get to the downhill edge while it is still the uphill edge*. While this is not always possible, it is always a possible aspiration.

Before proceeding further, let's establish that any mountain worthy of the term is comprised of two distinct parts: the groomed, or two-dimensional world of flatness; and everything else, the 3-D world of broken snow and untreated terrain that hosts a perpetual come-as-you-are party. In the 2-D domain, the weight shift that precipitates a change in direction is so elemental that even the tiniest children can master it. So what if in their mini-snowplow stances they may have one foot on the brakes while the other is on the gas? This apostasy from instructional scripture can be a useful skill in the 3-D realm. The little tykes still use a weighted, edged ski to turn and with that foundation they can go anywhere.

For people with a well-developed kinesthetic sense it should take all of two hours to learn how to make a carved turn on groomed terrain. We realize that there are people whose job it is to taffy-pull this process until it consumes decades, but let's presume benign, competent instruction that doesn't tie itself in knots of impenetrable terminology. The verbal part of the instruction might go something like this:

"As we stand here on the side of the hill, we naturally shift some extra weight to our downhill foot so we can stay comfortably in balance. Skiing is all about shifting weight from one foot to the other while remaining in balance, an action we normally call 'walking.' Skiing is actually easier than walking because there's no need to articulate the foot or stride with the legs. You can just stand there looking cute, but you do have to shift your weight from one foot to the other to make a turn.

"We want you to focus on your feet. As we start to glide across the hill, feel the pressure on the ball of your foot on the downhill ski. That pressure is what is holding your ski edge into the snow and guiding you on a secure line. Turning is easier when there is a little energy in the system so let's go a little faster. Keep your head up and look where you want to go so your body has some idea what you're intending. Point your feet where you want to go and as your skis start to drift in this new direction, shift as much weight as you can to the outside ski. This weight shift is accompanied by tilting the outside ski up on edge. To do this, just lift the pinky toe up on the outside ski so it's banked in the direction you want to travel. Keep the pressure on this ski until it has crossed over the fall line, then transfer your weight back to the opposite ski to turn back again. Repeat as necessary for the next 50 years."

Everything beyond this point is mere refinement and little tricks that help keep one centered and in balance. As you become comfortable with speed, you'll want to lean your body more into the turn and let your weight do most of the work in bending the ski into an arc. Dialing in the precise moment of weight shift is a lifelong pursuit; suffice it to say, the earlier in the turn one can apply pressure to an edged outside ski, the better. If you feel sluggish and late in making this weight shift, practice beginning each turn with a slight lift of what is to be the inside ski *from the heel*. (Never lift any ski up from the toe unless you like falling.) By picking this ski off the snow, all weight *has* to shift to the other ski; by picking it up from the heel, the upper body *has* to tip towards the inside of the turn. As long as you are carrying a minimum of speed, this move has to work every time.

The curious among you may wonder, if carving turns on groomed runs is so simple, how come somewhere north of 90% of all Americans are so dreadful at it? While it is impossible to assign percentages to each sub-set, we'd speculate that some skiers don't care about skills development as groomed terrain allows low-skill skiers to recreate without them; some have the kinesthetic awareness of fruit; some eschew all forms of self-education; and most think they are doing it right, at least part of the time. Oh well, as long as they're all happy, who cares?

The problem with not learning how to use both feet to carve a clean edge on groomers, aside from endangering yourself and those with whom you share the slope, is that until you clear this hurdle, the rest of the mountain, including the really, really good parts, is beyond your capabilities. Carving turns on groomers is the foundational skill upon which all other skills are based. Once you have the two-footed dance down on the ballroom floor, it's time to take your game to the rest of the mountain, where ecstasy lives.

Skiing powder, bumps and trees – sometimes all at once – is when skiing rises above sport to a transcendental plane where you become one with your movements. Skiing groomers is like learning scales; skiing the 3-D world is playing jazz. All the core concepts still apply: keep your torso quiet and square to your line of travel; stay centered, balanced and focused downhill; and work your two feet independently. But *how* you work your feet can be very different from what transpires on the groom. On groomage, your feet can remain planted, both to the bottom of the boot and to the slope. You can lift one or the other if the spirit moves you, but there's no need to in order to transition from turn to turn.

It's also possible to remain planted while slamming through all kinds of 3-D terrain, but you'd better have very fast, very educated feet. Once the snow gets deep enough so you can't feel the bottom, the business of keeping the feet planted at all times is closed until further notice. You have to keep your balance in a world that doesn't seem to have any equilibrium of its own. You have to be ready, willing and able to pick up either foot or both at any instant and move decisively. Now you don't just ski off the soles of your feet as you did on the groom, you use the whole foot - top, bottom and sides - pulling it out of one lumpy path and setting it on another. Instead of dancing the waltz, you cut a jitterbug trail. You take what the snow and the terrain propose and devise your own solution to the problem of descent. The niceties of carving take a back seat to the need to stay upright and in the flow.

There are many places on Snowbird to find trees, bumps and powder – the trifecta of off-piste skiing – but one of the more relentless shots that includes all three is Mach Schnell, right down the middle of the lower mountain. To take it from the top requires following the spine-collapsing whoop-de-dos of the Mid-Cirque Traverse to the dubious delights of the Ho Chi Min trail and thence to the aptly named Trail of Tears. When you finally run out of ridgeline to follow, Mach Schnell will lie directly below you, the top protected by tree glades that open to a short open section before choking down to solid, wall-to-wall moguls that fall to the canyon floor.

If you are going to charge this line, you cannot issue both feet the same assignment. One may have to complete a turn on its own while the other steps over to a fresh line with fewer immanent obstacles. Like the tiny tot in his two-footed snowplow, you may be obliged to brake with one foot while the other finds a slot in the fall line where it can fit. One thing is for sure: both feet are going to be very busy trying to make you look good.

When you see a gorgeous skier flying down terrain you wouldn't try to pick your way through, it may seem as though their legs are working as one. Not so, grasshopper. While there are moments in powder when your feet do move in lockstep, this isn't always possible. Usually, from moment to moment, one foot is dominant while the other functions as a safety chute in case of emergency, but both have to *move*, and move decisively. Independent leg action in 3-D terrain isn't so much a matter of technique as it is the result of staying in the flow, of moving as the terrain suggests and keeping everything else quiet but your busy feet. Independent foot action is also an attitude, a willingness to break form in order to achieve a higher goal. In the worst-case scenario, it's a survival technique, as when you whip around a left-hand corner and there's a berm 10 feet in front of you the size and shape of the Berlin Wall. You can't think your way through this problem, you have to act instinctively: extend the right leg to meet the Wall and conform to its non-conformable shape, pull the left leg under you so your upper body tilts momentarily away from the Wall, look ahead on your new axis of flight for an exit, now collapse the right leg and extend the left, tilting your foot against the face of the Wall and using your last ounce of momentum to arc over it as if it were a passing wave.

You can't pull off a maneuver like that if your feet aren't used to thinking independently and to some degree, thinking on their own. Almost everyone has an instinct for balance but not everyone trusts it. On skis, you have no other good options. You have to find your center and stay on it like it was the breath of life, which isn't all that hard once you learn to lean into the future, trust the prevailing forces of nature and let your feet find and define your fate,

Silver Fox, frosted over

Courtesy of Powder Shots

The Goo winging it at the top of Regulator Johnson

Blackjack Traverse, Peruvian Gulch

A path leads into Gad Valley

Chapter 21

On Paths

In our everyday lives, almost all paths are marked with boundaries, fixed edges we aren't supposed to breach. In the White World, there are also some well-defined paths, billiard-table smooth boulevards where you can push the speed envelope to the limit of imagination. But most paths here are unmarked, without clear borders. Your path becomes whatever you will it to be, a patchwork collage of turns that is uniquely yours.

What goes up must come down. This simple formula makes the magic of skiing possible. As we move through the up-and-down cycle, we both draw on and magnify the energy flow we've gathered here to help perpetuate. The lift system dictates how much energy we can store on our ascent, but it's left up to us to decide how to expend it properly on the way down. Gravity operates a theme park in every direction off Hidden Peak, and it's our job to find a way to ride it.

We must come down. While we can take any way down we wish, we can only take one way down at a time, so the choice of not just where to go but when is vitally important. This is never truer than on the first run, the baptism into that day's fire of opportunity.

Think big picture, how the layout of the giant hemispheres of Peruvian, Gad and Mineral faced the last blasts of wind and weather to roll over them, and how to find what you seek from this feast of options. Maybe what you need first is a jolt of speed, a head-clearing charge to dial you into the upper end of the flow rate. Perhaps the day-after wonders of High Baldy or the Road to Provo will open just as you reach the rope line, opening doorways to powder epiphanies with a lifespan shorter than mayflies. You might overhear a revelatory tram conversation that sends you, say, towards Eddie Mo's. But whatever path you choose, you need a plan.

You pick the path you pray will provide the conditions you seek. Your choice should be guided primarily by aspect, as wind, weather and exposure will affect the nearly 360° of choice presented by each of the mountain's sub-divisions differently. Suppose you suspect that north-facing slopes have the best chance of being soft. You still need to suss out which micro-aspect will hold the most snow, an intuition that can only be validated on site. And finally, you commit, take the sacrament of the path and accept the mountain's invitation to step into the stream.

The choice of path is a conscious calculation, the direction you intend to aim your arrow, an operation of wide-awake will. The business of aiming, the minutia of how to manage the line and the undulations the path presents, takes care of itself. Aiming happens at the subconscious level, the micro-choices best left to spontaneous, body-chosen reactions to stimuli. In any given arc along a certain path it may be necessary to add or subtract a little edge angle, toss your feet four more inches to the side or give the downhill ski a dash more pressure to pop out of the turn. These are choices, yes, and it's you making them, but they are reflexive responses, ingrained actions selected from an onboard menu of movements. This only happens when you're immersed in the event, being and doing lost in each others' embrace, the focus of your quiet consciousness on the path ahead, your energy one with the flow, your aim managed by the automatic instruments of intent.

A loose radical in the aiming equation is the influence of speed. Fickle handmaiden to both ease and effort, catalyst for crushing crud and siren of cataclysm in the cliffs, speed is a doorway to self-realization and, as Einstein warned us, a bender of time. Speed delivers the clarity of mystics, the expansion of the moment, the awareness that only comes from stillness, stillness that only appears at fifty miles an hour. The faster you go, the stiller it gets, until the energy of speed envelops you in the loudest quiet you've ever heard.

The mountain is always changing. The choice of path will evolve as the day progresses, conditions change, closed areas open and energy levels shift across the compass. To pick a representative path, let's imagine the latest blizzard followed the continent's customary atmospheric action and arrived from the west, slathering Peruvian Gulch in nine inches of accumulated essence. By 11:00 AM the easy pickings are gone, but a few lines will have escaped detection. Even the most travelled routes may hold unblemished shots on their borders, with main drag Chips the unexpected witness for the prosecution.

Off the cat-track that looks into Chips, drop in early and look for a seam along the trees, following the tree line on skier's left to find unexploited essence. When you meet the switchback road above Chip's Flats, hold onto your speed, take a high line to skier's right and catch the Shot 10 gate on Lower Baldy onto the Blackjack Traverse. Line after vulnerable line will materialize to your left, all short but fat, enticing you to commit early. If you have to go, then go, but greater wealth awaits those who wait. You are moving through an area that offers a Master's program from the University of Huck, so don't tarry under the plethora of precipices that dot the eastern rim of Peruvian Gulch. In other words, be observant of the uphill assault: fall-line sliders are hauling the mail out of the upper guts and you don't want to be the addressee.

As you move along this long traverse the question that hangs like hope in the air is, "Will the shot less trammeled be around the next shoulder, or should I commit now?" This is a question that can only be answered in the moment, but once you dive in and emerge a few elated turns later on Chips, look for the Blackjack Gate and cut back into the playground. Along this traverse all lines are generally equal, but those who stay closest to the trees and willows will harvest less picked pockets of goodness.

There are endless permutations on this run, as there are along every major artery on this infinitely mutable peak. No matter how often you ski it, the same path is never the same. Every detail changes from run to run, every descent finds its own variation, a fresh approach hidden in the seeming sameness. Familiarity of a given line develops the confidence to expand the boundaries of performance, a *Groundhog's Day* phenomenon where you remember the details so intimately, you can fold them into your story. Your familiarity with the mountain grows sharper and subtler. You find left-behind windows of self-indulgence, abandoned treasures only accessible to those who seek them out. And when you find them, you'll know you are where you are supposed to be, on the path that led you here.

To summarize, when it comes to picking the downward path, remember that wind carries weather; that timing and lighting are the most powerful variables governing the outcome; and most importantly, if you don't know where you're going, any road will get you there. However, when you choose your path with full intention, your focus on the moment will synchronize your flow with the vortex. When you become indistinguishable from your movement you become something holy, and in that moment you realize you are the Grail you seek.

Area served by the Blackjack Traverse

Everywhere People Ski

Freeride World Tour / Photographer: Jeremy Bernard
Oakley White-Allen scoping opportunities for self-expression

Chapter 22

On Self-Expression

At some point in every skier's life we reach a tipping point when we stop making turns and start making music. We migrate from being students whose highest achievement is perfect imitation, to masters who are elusively inimitable. When we make this passage, we acquire a signature style, a posture, an approach, an irreducible movement within a movement that is as unique as our fingerprints. Each run presents another opportunity for self-expression, a chance to use any crayon in the 48-color box, illustrating outside the lines all the way down the mountain.

What distinguishes this indulgence in self-celebration from any other form of hedonism? Because in this silly pursuit we seasonally redefine what is humanly possible. Not all of us, of course. The tip of the arrow is a space few can occupy at any one time. But the power propelling the sport forward moves us all, carrying everyone on its arc into the future. When Mike Lund threw the first Mobius flip in the 1970's, who could foresee the intricate aerial origami of a Bobby Brown four decades later? While the answer is no one, we can still trace a continuum from Lund to Brown, following a line that marks the boundary between the imagined and the achieved.

While only a handful of skiers in each generation will contribute to changing what is conceived as possible, all skiers can change what is possible for them. Just as with this little book of meditations, making the unseen manifest begins with the idea, the visualization of what lies just ahead. Skiing at the level of self-discovery is impossible without this ability to see what is invisible, not just in space, but in time, the moment as yet unlived. This is as true for the X Games aerialist who rotates like a gyroscope as it is for the World Cup downhiller running 85mph on injected ice. The future is a present we experience before the next heartbeat. Pulling ourselves artfully into the future is what self-expression is all about.

Self-expression always operates on three levels. The most basic self acts overly important, running the show at the conscious level, choosing what trick to throw where, which line to attack through the trees, etc. This is the level we normally think of as driving the bus, the fellow in charge, our loudmouth tour director. He picks the run, adjusts the speed, makes the linchpin move. But this primary level isn't what makes us unique, our self-expression separate from all others. That's more a function of level two, the unconscious, sympathetic nerve connections that define our style. The way we hold our poles. The forward curvature of our shoulders. The degree to which we commit our center to the turn. Our posture. These are habits that exist beyond conscious choice, free from critique and examination, a preset pattern as programmed as our DNA.

The level-two behaviors are telltale signs of what is operating below them and guiding their peculiarities, but they aren't themselves the undercurrent, the cause of causes, the impetus that fuels all expression. The power of self-expression emanates from a communion of our life force and that of the mountain. Level three is the awareness that the mountain has motives, that we are the agents of its self-expression as well as our own. Indeed, the mountain's voice is ours, the two as intertwined as a double helix, as inseparable as faith and hope.

When we make that first dive of intention, the post-trigger plunge into gravity's stream, we stop choosing a style. We do that which we do in the manner that we do it, an awkward definition for style, but we are beyond choosing one. Style *is* us, it's how we do what we find necessary to match the cadence of the mountain within the limits of our capabilities. When we disappear into our sensations, when we are our movements, when doing and being can no longer be pried apart, we stop controlling the idiosyncrasies that make us as unique as snowflakes; self-consciousness dissolves in a sea of ultra-consciousness, and in that transition identity emerges with more energy than it would ever have possessed by itself. Every contradiction is resolved in the moment when we disappear, the clock loses its stodgy grip on time and in the instant we evanesce we are never more ourselves.

No one can live forever on this edge. That's why it has been treated as sacred for thousands of years, longer than recorded time, longer than we could give expression to such awareness. The knowledge that we are both the anonymous water and the one-of-a-kind crystal, two opposite forms of perfection separated only by temperature, is just a transparent membrane away. We can no longer survive in this moment than shamans can live in the fire, but once we know it is there, we can never live without it.

Contrast this with the regular world where social convention keeps a tight rein on self-expression. We move only in approved ways and are only allowed to move with more abandon at sanctioned venues and events. If we moved through the everyday world the way a young jibber cavorts down Silver Fox, we'd be locked up. Whereas in the White World, we belong to a domain where personalized, idiosyncratic movement is intrinsic to the activity. It's dance or go home. There is still a need for etiquette and at least one law, that of gravity, but otherwise the only constraint on behavior is what the mountain will allow.

Riding in the flow of the vortex opens a channel to the inner self that allows it to surface. How we give voice to that expression is entirely up to us; there is no one else to filter it or judge it. We can express our communion with the flow of gravity, the curve of the mountain, the intoxication of speed and the medium of snow that facilitates this sublime activity any way that we want. This uncommon outpouring of soul is so intense that we can feel it even when we are removed from the White World. It can revisit us in our dreams and roll around in our imagination, allowing us to visualize the next time that we can be *there*, standing on the edge of gravity's stream.

And when we step into that stream, it's just us, baby. No one else is doing this but the buckaroo behind our eyeballs, the energy that wears our bodies like a space suit designed just so we can interface with the delicious dynamics of the gravity field. When we focus our energy on the immediate future we move into it, seeing ourselves joining the quantum field of possibilities, clarifying an image of our future selves so that when our movements blossom into the present, they are as perfect as our vision.

Technology is how humans augment their capacity for self-expression, which is how we have skiing in the first place. In the late 1800's, miners would slide on 15-foot pine slabs, controlling their speed with a single pole between the legs. As technique and equipment improved, movements became more supple and skilled, letting sliders explore more interesting forms of self-expression. The efficiency with which we now transport ourselves both uphill and down has exploded the limits of possibility. Super-fat skis, twin tips and snowboards have pushed the previous parameters of self-expression into new realms, enabling wild, exquisite assaults on Alaskan faces so steep they shouldn't be able to hold snow.

The same tools that enable elite athletes to execute the impossible also assist those less adventurous to find their own highest expression. We can fire at fall lines that used to intimidate, ride backwards on a whim, pirouette on the head of a pin or carve flawless arcs anywhere. We can use our new freedom of movement to be aggressive or delicate, hug the fall line or swoop across it. We toy with the power of the vortex, match our movements to contours of the mountain, allow its energy to be ours.

Nothing moves the entire art of self-expression forward quite like the addition of new selves to the mix. Here's to Stein Eriksen,

Wayne Wong, Scot Schmidt, Doug Coombs, Shane McConkey, Johnny Moseley, Seth Morrison and all the other geniuses who wouldn't settle for the status quo. Here's to the kids building a kicker in a Midwestern hayfield, honing their vision and their skills without fanfare or applause, just for the bliss of it. When all that enthusiasm finally finds its way to a big mountain like Snowbird, fresh eyes see launch platforms off every terrain feature. As they revel in a world of new possibilities, the mountain must feel like a fine, old instrument in the hands of young prodigies.

For as all who come here must confess, it was the mountain who called them here, who enlisted their energy and self-expression to feed its battery and enhance its energy flow. Just as the mountain imports skiers for its purposes, in return it buries within each of its acolytes the invitation to take its energy home. If we only remember to unwrap the gift, we will find within it, within ourselves, the meaning of a life well lived.

Thank you!

Disclaimer

All skiing involves an element of risk. Skiing expert terrain increases these inherent risks. We are not encouraging anyone to ski beyond his or her physical abilities and we definitely do not condone skiing out of control in any circumstances. We caution all skiers to know their limits and respect their fellow skiers' desires for a safe and enjoyable experience.

About the Authors

Jackson Hogen has played more roles in the ski trade than Eskimos have words for snow: ski designer, binding and boot product manager, freestyle competitor, retail salesman, lecturer on risk management, ski instructor, marketing director, resort feature writer, ski tester for 25 years and boot tester for 20, OLN and RSN television show host, extreme camp ski coach, Desperate Measures co-creator, 4X Warren Miller screenwriter, R&D chief, honorary Canadian, college racer, 2X personal therapist to Greg Stump, regular contributor to at least ten different ski magazines (whore), and in his guise as Pontiff of Powder, married Paul Hochman and Carrie Sheinberg in all ways but legally.

The mountain called **"Guru" Dave Powers** here in 1976 and he's plumbed its slopes for an average of 130 days a season ever since. The Goo doesn't just understand every aspect of Snowbird's constantly changing conditions; he lives them. He shares his knowledge in a daily blog, www.gurudavepowers.com with tens of thousands of adherents. Powers has a gift for seeing connections most of us ignore, a talent he has applied to deepening his 36-year relationship with this mountain. *Snowbird Secrets* draws on Powers' detailed experience of every millimeter of this mountain while it illuminates the themes that forever bind him here.

CPSIA information can be obtained at www.ICGtesting.com
Printed in the USA
BVOW11s0530160215

387732BV00004B/6/P